GOOD WOOD HANDBOOK

ALBERT JACKSON · DAVID DAY
DESIGNED BY SIMON JENNINGS

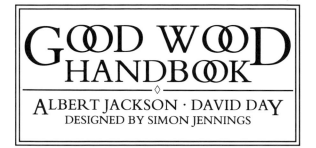

GOOD WOOD HANDBOOK

◇

ALBERT JACKSON · DAVID DAY

DESIGNED BY SIMON JENNINGS

BETTERWAY PUBLICATIONS

WOOD COLOUR REPRODUCTION
The natural colour of wood can vary considerably, not only in the
same species but also in the same tree. Moreover, the direction of light
has an effect on the perceived colour of the wood. Every effort has
been made in this book to reproduce the natural colour of each
species within the limitations of the printing process.

Text
Albert Jackson
David Day

Design
Simon Jennings

Text editor
Peter Leek

Illustrators
David Day
Robin Harris

Photography
Neil Waving

Typesetting
Chambers Wallace

First published in 1991 by
HarperCollins Publishers
London
Reprinted 1992, 1993

First published in the USA by
Betterway Publications,
an imprint of F & W Publications, Inc.,
1507 Dana Ave, Cincinnati, Ohio 45207.
Reprinted 1993

This book was created exclusively for
HarperCollins Publishers by
Jackson Day Jennings Ltd trading as
Inklink.

The text and illustrations on pages 8-17,
19-21, 43, 99-103, 113-116, and in the
Glossary of terms were previously published in
Collins Complete Woodworker's Manual.
All other text and illustrations are
original to this book.

Copyright © 1991
HarperCollins Publishers Ltd

ISBN 1-55870-274-1

Printed in Hong Kong

INTRODUCTION

THE NATURE OF WOOD is such that a stack of timber cut from one single species can reveal a bewildering variety of grain pattern, colour and tone depending on where the tree was grown and from which part of that tree the wood was cut. Add to this complexity the number of species of wood you could expect to find in any good timber yard and one begins to appreciate why the average wood-worker finds it difficult to tell one wood from another. Identification aside, how does a wood user decide which of all these timbers will best suit his or her needs?

This pocket book is a guide to identifying and choosing wood from a selection of some of the world's commercial softwoods and hard-woods. Each species is described in detail and shown in three dimensions, plus an actual-size view of its grain and the effect of a clear finish upon its colour. You can even identify the trees themselves with the help of full-colour illustra-tions. Examples of decorative veneers and man-made boards are also included.

When selecting a particular wood, no concerned wood user can any longer ignore the fact that certain species represent a diminish-ing resource. This book will enable you to identify those species most at risk and either choose an alternative or ensure the wood you are buying comes from a sustainable source.

ALBERT JACKSON & DAVID DAY

ACKNOWLEDGMENTS

INKLINK are grateful to the following individuals,
companies and organizations for their generous
contributions and assistance.

For the supply and preparation of the woods, veneers
and man-made boards illustrated in this book:
C.F. Anderson & Son Ltd, London, N1
Annandale Timber & Moulding Co. Pty, Ltd, N.S.W., Aus.
The Art Veneer Co. Ltd, Mildenhall, Suffolk.
John Boddy's Fine Wood & Tool Store Ltd, N.Yorks.
Jim Cummins, Woodstock, N.Y.
Desfab, Beckenham, Kent.
Egger (U.K.) Ltd, Hexham, Northumberland.
FIDOR, Feltham, Middlesex.
General Woodworking Supplies, London, N16.
Highland Forest Products PLC., Inverness-shire.
E. Jones & Son, Erith, Kent.
Limehouse Timber, Dunmow, Essex.
Ravensbourne College of Design & Communication, Kent.
Seaboard International Ltd, London, SW1.
F. R. Shadbolt, London, E4.
Fred Spalding, Bromley, Kent.

For the supply of information and reference material:
American Plywood Association, European Div. London, W1.
Association of Woodusers Against Rainforest Exploitation, London, N5.
Australian Particleboard Research Institute, Inc. N.S.W.
Stuart Batty, Buxton, Derbyshire.
Buckinghamshire College of Higher Education, High Wycombe, Bucks.
Council of Forest Industries of British Columbia, U.K. office, London, SW15.
Craft Supplies Ltd, Buxton, Derbyshire.
Fastnet Products Ltd, Chard, Somerset.
Finnish Plywood International, Welwyn Garden City, Herts.
Walter Fischer, Kassel, W.Germany.
Friends of the Earth Ltd. London, N1.
Furniture Industry Research Association, Stevenage, Herts.
Louisiana-Pacific Corporation, Portland, Oregon.
Theodor Nagel (G.M.B.H. & Co.), D2 Hamburg 28, Germany.
Overseas Development Natural Resources Institute, Chatham, Kent.
The Oxford Forestry Institute, Oxford.
Plywood Association of Australia Ltd, Newstead, QLD.
Royal Botanic Gardens, Kew, Surrey.
Timber Development Association (N.S.W.) Ltd, Australia.
Timber Research and Development Association, High Wycombe, Bucks,
with special thanks for providing Timbers of the World Red Booklets 1-9 for reference.
Timber Trade Federation, London, W1.
U.S. Forest Products Laboratory, Madison, Wisconsin I.
Verein Deutscher Holzeinfuhrhäuser e.V. Hamburg, Germany.

Also thanks to special consultants:
Jim Cummins – U.S. consultant.
Les Reed – Veneers and marquetry materials.
Illustrations P8-9 by Michael Woods.

CONTENTS

How Trees Grow

Trees are undeniably a valuable source of wealth, but they are not valuable in the same way gold is. Although it could be argued that wood is as beautiful and desirable as any precious metal, the great value of trees lies in their being a renewable resource. Nor, historically, has any other material been so adaptable and of such immeasurable benefit to mankind as wood with its infinite variety of types and uses.

THE LIVING TREE

In order to appreciate the properties of wood and how it is worked and finished, it is worthwhile understanding something of the way trees grow.

Trees form an important division of the plant kingdom known as the Spermatophyta (seed-bearing plants). This division is subdivided into Gymnospermae and Angiospermae. Gymnosperms are needle-leaved coniferous trees commonly referred to as softwoods. Angiosperms are broadleaved trees known as hardwoods and may be either deciduous or evergreen.

Leaf-bearing branches
The leaves produce nutrients to feed the tree by photosynthesis.

Trunk
The trunk supports the leaf-bearing branches and is the main source of wood.

Root system
The roots that anchor the tree also absorb water and minerals from the ground.

Angiosperms
Broadleaved trees.

The structure of a tree
A typical tree has a main stem, known as the bole or trunk, which carries a crown of leaf-bearing branches. A root system anchors the tree in the ground and absorbs water and minerals to sustain the tree. The trunk carries the sap from the roots via the cell system to the leaves.

Food storage
Evaporation from the leaves draws the sap through minute cells which form the structure of the tree. Carbon dioxide in the air is taken in by the tree through pores in the leaves known as stomata. The food produced by the leaves is dispersed to the growing parts of the tree as well as being stored by some of the cells.

Photosynthesis
Photosynthesis (a reaction of organic compounds from carbon dioxide and water) takes place when energy in the form of light is absorbed by chlorophyll, the green pigment present in leaves, to produce the nutrients on which a tree lives. As a by-product of this process, oxygen is given off to the atmosphere.

The structure of wood
Wood is a mass of cellulose tubular cells bonded together with an organic chemical called lignin. The cells vary in size and shape, but are generally long and thin and run longitudinally with the main axis of the tree's trunk or branches. It is this orientation of the cells that produces the direction of the grain.

Cells provide support for the tree, circulation of sap and food storage. Softwoods or conifers have a simple cell structure composed mainly of tracheid (fibrelike) cells which provide initial sap conduction and physical support. They form regular radiating rows and make up the main body of the tree.

Hardwoods or deciduous trees have fewer tracheids than softwoods and have vessels or pores that conduct sap and fibres which provide support. It is this cell specialization that enables cut wood to be identified as a softwood or hardwood. The size and distribution of the cells vary from species to species, producing fine-textured or coarse-textured wood.

A tree grows by an annual deposition of cells formed by the cambium layer. This is the thin layer of active living cells between the bark and the wood. During the growing period the cells subdivide to form new wood on the inner side and phloem or bast (tissue that conducts synthesized food to all parts of the plant) on the outside.

As the girth of the tree increases, the old bark splits and new bark is formed. The new wood cells develop into specialized cells to form sapwood. Sapwood is made up partly of living food-storage cells and partly of non-living cells which are capable of conducting sap up the tree and do not store food. In addition to cells following the axis of the trunk, there are ray cells radiating from the centre of the tree. These carry and store nutrients horizontally through the sapwood. Ray cells form flat vertical bands which are hardly visible in softwoods but plainly obvious in some hardwoods, such as oak, particularly when they are quarter-sawn.

As the tree grows, a new ring of sapwood is built up around the previous year's growth. The oldest sapwood is now no longer used to conduct water, and gradual chemical changes convert it into heartwood to form the structural spine of the tree. In this way the heartwood increases in area, while the thickness of the sapwood remains relatively constant throughout the tree's life.

Gymnosperms
Needle-leaved trees.

9

Sapwood and heartwood

Sapwood is light in colour and is usually recognizable by its contrast with the darker heartwood. The colour difference is not so marked on light-coloured woods, particularly the softwoods. Sapwood is inferior to heartwood and is usually cut to waste by furniture-makers. It is not so resistant to fungal decay, and it is also prone to beetle attack because of the carbohydrates stored in some of the cells. The relatively thin-walled cells are porous and give up moisture quickly. As a result, sapwood shrinks more than the denser heartwood. However, its porosity allows stains and preservatives to be readily absorbed.

Since heartwood is the inner part of the maturing tree and is formed from old sapwood, it plays no active part in the growth of the tree. Hence the dead cells can become blocked with organic material, causing the cell walls to change colour through the presence of chemical substances called extractives. The extractives are responsible for the rich colours found in many hardwoods. They also impart a measure of resistance to fungus and insect attack.

Earlywood and latewood

As with many plants, the way trees grow depends on climatic conditions. In a temperate climate there is generally rapid growth in the spring, less in summer and no new growth in winter.

Earlywood or springwood is, as the name implies, the part of the annual growth ring laid down in the early part of the growing season. Thin-walled tracheid cells in softwoods and open tube-like vessels in hardwoods form the bulk of the earlywood to facilitate the rapid conduction of sap. Earlywood can usually be recognized as the wider band of paler-coloured wood in each annual growth ring.

Latewood or summerwood is the part of the annual ring that develops in the latter part of the growing season and produces thicker-walled cells, creating denser and usually darker wood which is less able to conduct sap but adds support to the tree.

This distinct banding corresponds to one season's growth, so reveals the age of the felled tree and the kind of climatic conditions in which it has grown. Wide annual rings indicate good growing conditions, narrow ones poor or drought conditions.

The difference in texture between earlywood and latewood is of importance to the woodworker since it can render a wood more or less difficult to work. The lighter-weight earlywood is easier to cut than the denser latewood. This is not a particular problem for most hand and machine processes, provided the tools' cutting edges are sharp. However, the difference in hardness can show where

Cambium layer
A thin layer of living cell tissue that forms the new wood and bark.

Sapwood
The new wood, the cells of which conduct or store nutrients.

Heartwood
The mature wood that forms the spine of the tree.

Pith
The central core of cells. Often weak and suffers from fungus attack.

Phloem or bast
The inner bark tissue that conducts synthesized food.

Growth ring
The layer of wood which is formed in on growing period. Large earlywood and smaller latewood cells make up the annual growth ring.

latewood is left proud of earlywood after finishing with a sander. Generally, woods with even-textured growth rings are the easiest to work and finish.

The distribution of hardwood cells has a marked effect on the texture of the wood. 'Ring-porous' hardwoods such as oak or ash have clearly defined rings of large vessels in the earlywood, and dense fibres and cell tissue in the latewood. These woods are more difficult to finish than 'diffuse-porous' woods, such as beech, which have vessels and fibres distributed relatively evenly. Although woods like mahogany are often diffuse-porous, their larger cells can make them coarse-textured.

Earlywood and latewood

Ring-porous wood

Diffuse-porous wood

Ray cells
Radiating sheets of cells that conduct nutrients horizontally, also known as 'medullary rays'.

Bark
The outer protective layer of dead cells. The term can also include the living inner tissue.

13

CONVERTING WOOD

It takes many years, hundreds in the case of some species, for a tree to grow to a commercially viable size. Yet with modern forestry methods straight-growing trees such as pine can be cut down, topped and debarked in a matter of minutes. Since conifers are relatively fast-growing, with careful husbandry it is possible to control supply and demand of softwoods. It is a sad fact, however, that the forests of the world are being depleted – particularly of the slow-growing hardwoods, which are becoming increasingly scarce, though most specialist suppliers stock small pieces of exotic woods.

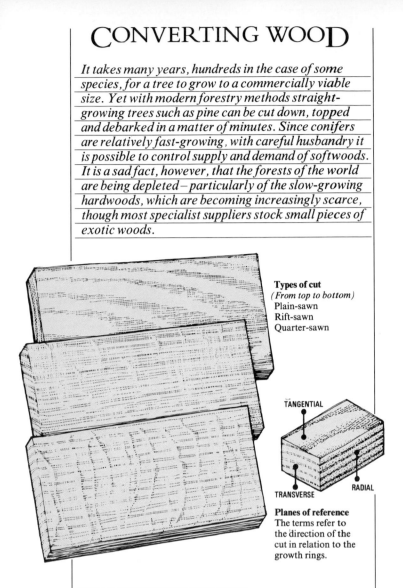

Types of cut
(From top to bottom)
Plain-sawn
Rift-sawn
Quarter-sawn

TANGENTIAL

TRANSVERSE

RADIAL

Planes of reference
The terms refer to
the direction of the
cut in relation to the
growth rings.

THE CONVERSION PROCESS

Most commercial wood is cut from the trunk of the tree. Some larger limbs may also be cut into logs, but branch material usually has asymmetric growth rings that produce unstable 'reaction' wood, which warps and splits easily. Reaction wood is formed in limbs or trunks which do not grow upright. In soft-woods the growth is mainly on the underside and produces 'compression wood'; in hardwoods it forms on the upper side and is known as 'tension wood'.

Felled trees are cut into logs or butts and transported to local sawmills for conversion into rough-sawn timber; the trimmings are usually made into paper products and manu-factured boards. Exporters of timber may deal in whole or sawn logs, or both. But the producers of some exotic hard-woods, in Peninsular Malaysia, Indonesia, the Philippines and Brazil, for example, now trade in sawn wood only. This is in a quest to protect their trees from overcutting and also to provide employment for their people and an increase in revenue. The top-quality logs with large even boles command high prices and are usually converted into veneer.

Milling

Today most logs are converted into sawn timber by band-saw or circular-saw machines. Before the machine age this task was achieved by hand. A large two-man saw was used, with one sawyer in a pit below the log and the other standing on top of it. Pushing and pulling the saw between them, they would gradually convert the log into boards or beams.

The main types of cut produced by modern methods are known as 'plain-sawn' and 'quarter-sawn'. Plain-sawn boards are broadly those where the growth rings meet the face of the board at an angle of less than 45 degrees. Quarter-sawn is broadly defined as timber which has the growth rings at not less than 45 degrees to the face of the board.

Within both these categories other terms may be used. Plain-sawn timber can be known as flat-sawn, flat-grain or slash-sawn; and quarter-sawn as rift-sawn, comb-grain, edge-grain and vertical-grain.

In America, plain-sawn boards are those where the growth rings meet the face at an angle of less than 30 degrees. Those where the rings meet at more than 30 degrees but at less than 60 degrees are known as rift-sawn boards.

True quarter-sawn boards are cut radially with the annual rings perpendicular to the board's face, but in practice all boards with rings at an angle of not less than 60 degrees are classified as quarter-sawn.

Plain-sawn boards are cut on a tangent to the annual-growth rings and display a decorative and distinctive elliptical figure.

Rift-sawn boards display a straight figure with some ray-cell patterning, and are sometimes referred to as comb-grain.

Quarter-sawing reveals a straight figure crossed with ray-fleck figure found in hardwoods such as oak.

Converting a log

The stability and figure of the wood are determined by the plane of the saw in relation to the annual growth rings. The most economical method for converting a log is to cut it 'through and through' (1). This process makes parallel cuts through the length of the log and produces plain-sawn, rift-sawn and a small percentage of quarter-sawn boards. Plain-sawn logs are cut partly through and through, and produce a mixture of plain-sawn and rift-sawn boards (2).

Converting a log to produce quarter-sawn boards can be done in a number of ways. The ideal is to cut each board parallel with the rays, like the radiating spokes of a wheel, but this method is wasteful and not used commercially. The conventional method, albeit a compromise, is to cut the log into quarters and then cut each quadrant into boards (3). Commercial quarter-sawing first cuts the log into thick slices, which are then converted into boards (4).

To select quarter-sawn wood, look at the end grain. Choose boards which have the growth rings at about 90 degrees to the surface.

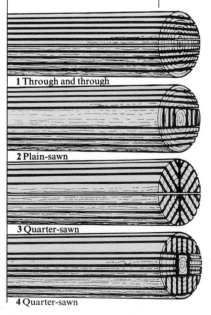

1 Through and through

2 Plain-sawn

3 Quarter-sawn

4 Quarter-sawn

DRYING WOOD

Green wood newly cut from a log contains a very high percent-age of moisture. The cell walls are saturated and free water is held by the cell cavities. Drying or 'seasoning' wood is the process of removing the free water and much of the bound moisture from the cell walls. As the wood dries, free water is lost from the cell cavities until only the cell walls contain moisture. This is known as the fibre-saturation point and occurs at about 30 per cent moisture content, depending on species. It is when moisture starts to be lost from the cell walls that shrinkage begins. The loss of water will stop when it is in balance with the relative humidity of its surroundings. This is known as the equilibrium moisture content (EMC).

It is most important that the seasoning process is carried out properly, in order to prevent stresses being created within the wood and to ensure that the EMC is at the appropriate level to avoid problems with swelling and shrinkage.

Air-drying

Air-drying is the traditional method for seasoning wood. The boards are stacked evenly on spacer battens, or 'stickers', which are 25mm (1in) square and are spaced 450mm (1ft 6in) apart. The stacks are usually built well clear of the ground in a sheltered position and are protected from rain and direct sunlight. The natural airflow through the stack gradually dries the wood. As a rough guide, it takes about one year to dry every 25mm (1in) thickness for hardwoods and about half that time for softwoods.

This method is inexpensive but can only reduce the moisture content to about 14 to 16 per cent, depending on the relative humidity. For interior use, the wood needs further drying in a kiln or is left to dry naturally in the environment in which it is to be used.

Kiln-drying

Wood for interior use needs a moisture content of about 8 to 10 per cent, or possibly lower, depending on the humidity of the location.

Kiln-drying is used com-mercially to reduce the moisture content of the wood below air-dry level, and only takes a matter of days. The boards are loaded onto trolleys in stickered stacks and rolled into the kiln, where a care-fully controlled mixture of hot air and steam is pumped through the piled wood and the humidity is gradually reduced to a specified moisture content according to the species of wood being dried. Wood dried below air-dry level will try to take up moisture if left exposed – so, where possible, keep kiln-dried wood in the environment in which it is to be used.

Checking moisture content

The moisture content of wood is given as a percentage of its oven-dry weight. This is calculated by comparing the original weight of a sample block (preferably taken from the centre of the board rather than the end) with the weight of the sample after it has been fully dried in an oven. The dry weight is subtracted from the original weight to determine the weight loss, and the following equation used to calculate the moisture-content percentage:

$$\frac{\text{Weight of water lost from sample}}{\text{Oven-dry weight of sample}} \times 100$$

Moisture meters with two-pin electrodes are a simple and convenient way to check the moisture content. The meter measures the resistance of the moist wood and gives an instant reading of the moisture-content percentage.

Insert the electrodes into the wood at various points along the board to check the average level, as not all parts of the board dry at the same rate.

BUILDING-BLOCK WEIGHTS

STICKERS

COVER

Air-drying at home
Construct an even stack of 'stickered' boards for air to pass through.

BUILDING-BLOCK SUPPORTS

WOODEN BEAMS

BOARDS

Stability
When wood dries, it shrinks. The shape of the board can change or 'move' as shrinkage takes place. In general, the shrinkage along the line of the annual rings amounts to approximately twice the shrinkage across them. Tangentially cut plain-sawn boards therefore shrink more in their width. Quarter-sawn boards shrink only slightly in their width and very little in their thickness.

Shrinkage movement can also cause some distortion. The concentric growth rings of a tangentially cut plain-sawn board run approxi- mately edge to edge and differ in length. The longer outer rings shrink more than the inner rings, resulting in a tendency for the board to bend, or 'cup', across its width. Square sections of wood are liable to become parallelograms, and round sections to become oval.

The growth rings of a quartered board run from face to face and, being virtually the same length, suffer little or no distortion. This stability, coupled with an even-wearing surface, makes quartered boards the preferred type for flooring and furniture-making.

Shrinkage movement
Sections of wood will distort differently depending on orientation of the growth rings.

Commercial air-drying
Sawn boards, spaced apart with stickers, are placed on pallets and set in huge stacks at the mill.

SELECTING WOOD

*Timber suppliers usually stock spruce, fir and pine,
the softwoods most commonly used for carpentry and
joinery. These woods are generally sold as 'dimension' or 'dressed' stock – that is, as sawn or surface-
planed sections cut to standard sizes. One or more of
the faces may be surfaced. Note that the planing
process can remove at least 3mm ($\frac{1}{8}$in) from each
face of the wood, making the actual width and thickness less than the 'sawn size' quoted by the timber
merchant. The length, on the other hand, is always
as quoted. Although the majority of hardwoods are
generally sold as boards of random width and length,
certain types of mahogany, teak, oak and ramin can
be bought as dimension stock. Dimension timber is
sold by the foot or in 300mm units. Check which
system your supplier uses, as the metric unit is about
5mm ($\frac{3}{16}$in) shorter than an imperial foot. Always
allow extra on the length for waste.*

Shakes
are splits that occur in
the structure of the wood
due to growth defects or
shrinkage stresses. Cup
or ring shakes are splits
that open between the
annual-growth rings.

Honeycomb checks
occur inside the board
when the outside
stabilizes before the
inside is dry. The
inside shrinks more
than the outside, which
usually results in torn
internal fibres.

Surface checking
usually occurs along
the rays, and is usually
caused by rapid drying
of the surface.

End splits
are common and are
caused by rapid drying
of the exposed end.
Sealing the ends with
waterproof paint can
prevent splitting.

Bowing or warping
is caused by stacking
boards badly and
introduces stresses
which make the wood
difficult to cut.
'Reaction' wood is
also prone to cast when
dried or cut.

16

Grading
Softwoods are graded for evenness of grain and amount of allowable defects such as knots. The better-quality 'appearance grades' and 'non-stress grades' are probably of most interest to the general woodworker. Stress-graded softwoods are rated for structural use where strength is important. The term 'clear timber' is often used for knot-free or defect-free wood, but this kind of timber is not usually available from suppliers unless specified.

The grading of hardwoods is determined by the area of defect-free wood. The greater the area, the higher the grade. The best grades are 'firsts' and 'firsts and seconds' (FAS).

Many specialist firms will supply wood by mail order – but whenever possible, select the wood yourself. When you go to buy wood, take a block plane with you so you can plane a small sample if the colour and grain are obscured by dirt or by sawing.

WOOD DEFECTS

Unless wood is dried carefully, stresses can be introduced which mar it or make it difficult to work. Insufficient drying can lead to shrinkage of dimensioned parts, joints opening, and warping and splitting.
Before buying wood, check the surface for splits, knots and uneven grain. Look at the end-section to identify the cut from the log and any distortion. Sight along the length to check for twisting or bowing.

Bow

Twist or wind

Spring

Ingrown bark can mar the appearance and weaken the structure of the wood.

Cutting lists
Before ordering materials from a timber supplier, write a cutting list which specifies the length, width and thickness of every component in a workpiece. The list should also state the material from which each component is to be made and the quantity required. Make sure your supplier is aware that the list specifies finished sizes so that he or she knows how much to allow for wastage.

Dead or encased knots are the remains of dead branches, the stumps of which are overgrown by new growth rings.

17

ABBREVIATIONS AND DEFINITIONS

Timber merchants have evolved their own jargon which is often abbreviated in catalogues and price lists. The following list gives the typical terminology used in the timber trade.

BD FT
Board foot. A unit of volume $12 \times 12 \times 1$in (144in^3)

CLR (Clear)
Wood that is free from knots and other defects.

CLS
Canadian Lumbar Standard relating to spruce, pine and fir.

Common
American hardwood-grading term with four or five subdivisions.

EMC
Equilibrium moisture content. The moisture content a piece of timber will ultimately reach when exposed to a more or less constant level of temperature and humidity.

FAS
Firsts and seconds. The best American grade for hardwoods.

F1F
An American grade for hardwoods with one FAS face and one No 1 common, or better.

FR
Foot run. A term used in calculating the price (usually of softwoods).

FS
Fresh-sawn. Wood supplied newly cut from the log.

ft, ft^2, ft^3
Feet, square feet, cubic feet.

HG
Home-grown.

in, ins
Inch, inches.

KD
Kiln-dried. Timber dried artificially to a lower moisture content and more quickly than can be achieved by air drying.

Kg
Kilogramme.

MC
Moisture content. The proportion (by weight) of water present in the tissues of a piece of timber, given as a percentage of the oven-dry weight.

Nominal dimensions
The standardized widths and thicknesses of timber when newly sawn from the log. Also, used to refer to the various sections thereafter. The actual sizes will subsequently be reduced by shrinkage and planing.

1SE
One square edge. A board having one edge cut square, the other being left with sapwood and bark.

PAR
Planed all round. Wood that has had all sides planed after dimension sawing.

PBS
Planed both sides.

Per cube
A term used in pricing timber where the cost of a cubic foot is quoted.

PS
Part seasoned. Some dense woods are difficult to season and are sold as part seasoned with no guarantee as to the moisture content.

SE (Squares)
Boards which are cut square on both edges.

Selects
The second-best American grade.

SFM
Super feet measure. The surface area expressed in square feet.

SPF
Spruce pine fir. These woods are grouped together because they have similar properties and are marketed as a single species.

T & G
Tongued and grooved. Having a tongue machined into one edge and a groove in the other.

TT
Through and through. The process of cutting a log through its full length and width with parallel cuts, producing boards with sapwood and bark on both edges.

Wane
The untrimmed edge of a board showing sapwood and bark.

THE PROPERTIES OF WOOD

Since wood is a product of nature, each piece is unique. Each section of wood taken from a tree, or even from the same board, will be different. It may have the same strength or colour, but not the same grain pattern. It is this diversity of character, strength, colour, workability and even scent that makes wood so appealing to woodworkers. Working wood is a learning process, and each piece of wood is a challenge to the worker's skills. Only by handling wood and experiencing the way it behaves can a full appreciation of its properties be gained. The natural characteristics of wood are briefly set out below, and different kinds of wood from all over the world are illustrated on the following pages.

NATURAL CHARACTERISTICS

The appearance of wood – the grain pattern, colour and texture – is the prime consideration when choosing wood for a project. Its working or strength characteristics are usually a secondary consideration, but they are no less important and the wood must also be selected for fitness of purpose. If you are not familiar with a particular wood which appeals to you, discuss its properties with your supplier to make sure it will suit your requirements.

Selecting wood is a process of balancing appearance with strength, workability, pliability, weight, cost and availability. The appearance and characteristics of wood are determined by the nature of its cell structure.

Grain

The mass of the wood's cell structure constitutes the 'grain' of the wood, which follows the main axis of the tree's trunk, and the nature of the grain is determined by the disposition and degree of orientation of these longitudinal cells.

Trees which grow straight and even produce 'straight-grained' wood. 'Cross-grained' wood is formed where the cells deviate from the main axis of the tree. Some trees twist as they grow and produce 'spiral grain'. In some instances the spiral growth veers from one angle to another, with each change taking place over a few growth rings; this results in 'interlocked grain'. 'Wavy grain' and 'curly grain' occur in trees that have an undulating cell structure; the former has short even waves, the latter is irregular.

Irregular-grained woods can be difficult to work and finish, as the cells constantly change direction, creating 'wild grain'.

Boards with random or undulating grain display various patterns according to the angle to the surface and light-reflectivity of the cell structure. These effects are exploited in the production of veneers.

The term grain is also used in referring to the way wood is cut or worked. Sawing 'with the grain' refers to cuts made along the length of the wood, that is with the longitudinal cells.

Planing a surface 'with the grain' follows the direction of the grain where the fibres are parallel or slope up and away from the direction of the cutting action. This results in a smooth trouble-free cut.

Planing 'against the grain' refers to cuts made where the fibres slope up and towards the direction of the planing action, producing a rough cut.

Sawing or planing 'across the grain' refers to cuts made more or less perpendicular to the grain.

Figure

The term grain is commonly used to describe the appearance of wood, but what is really being referred to is a combination of natural growth features collectively known as the 'figure'.

The difference in growth between the earlywood and latewood, the density of the annual growth rings, the concentricity or eccentricity of the rings, the distribution of colour, the effect of disease or physical damage and the method used to convert the wood into boards all contribute to the figure.

Most trees produce conically shaped trunks which when cut tangentially produce typical plain-sawn boards displaying a U-shaped pattern where the layers of annual growth rings are exposed by the plane of the cut. When a log is cut radially or quarter-sawn the annual rings are perpendicular to the plane of cut and the figure is less distinctive, showing a series of parallel lines. Some woods, however, have distinctive ray cells which are exposed by quarter-sawing and produce an attractive 'ray-fleck' figure.

The form of the figure is not restricted to wood from straight trunks. The fork formed by a branch and the main stem of the tree produces 'curl' or 'crotch' figure much prized as veneer, as is burr wood which is an abnormal growth caused by some injury. Stumpwood also yields interesting random-grain figure which, like burr, can be used for turning work.

Texture

The term 'texture' refers to the relative size of the wood's cells. Fine-textured woods have small closely spaced cells, whilst coarse-textured woods have relatively large cells. 'Texture' is also used to describe the distribution of the cells in relation to the annual growth rings. Where the difference between earlywood and latewood is slight the wood is even-textured, whereas wood with marked contrast in the growth rings has an uneven texture.

IDENTIFYING WOOD

Some common woods can be readily identified by their grain, colour, texture and smell. However, unfamiliar woods can be extremely difficult to identify – and even experts sometimes have to resort to microscopic analysis of the cell structure.

The following pages illustrate in colour a selection of commercial woods from around the world. Each wood is referred to by its standard name and, where appropriate, its commercial or local names are included.

The genus and species are given in italics. These are all important, since the botanical name is the only universal classification that can be relied on to identify a species of wood accurately. In reference books and suppliers' catalogues the term 'sp.' or 'spp.' is commonly used to indicate that a wood may be one of a variety of species within a genus, or 'family', of trees.

The level of durability of the woods described here relates to their performance when in contact with soil. Perishable wood is rated at less than 5 years, very durable at more than 25 years. Durability can vary according to the level of exposure and climatic conditions.

Most woods darken with exposure to light, though some lighten or even change colour. Applied finishes, no matter how clear, tend to darken the colour of wood. The following softwoods and hardwoods include small square samples to show the wood, actual size, before and after the application of a clear finish.

The term softwood refers to the botanical grouping of the wood rather than its physical properties. Softwoods come from coniferous trees, which belong to the botanical group Gymnospermae (plants that bear exposed seeds). Most cone-bearing trees are evergreen and have narrow, needle-shaped leaves. The standing tree is commonly depicted as having a tall, pointed outline – but not all conifers are this shape. When converted into boards, softwoods are readily identified by their relatively light colour range, from pale yellow to reddish brown, and by the grain pattern created by the contrast in colour and density between the earlywood and latewood in the annual growth rings.

Distribution of softwoods
■ Coniferous forest
■ Coniferous and broadleaved deciduous mixed forest

The softwood regions of the world
The prime source of the world's supply of commercial softwoods is the northern hemisphere, which extends across the arctic and subarctic regions of Europe and North America down to the southeastern United States.

Conifers are relatively fast-growing, producing straight trunks which can be economically cultivated and harvested in man-made forests. They are cheaper than hardwoods and widely used for building construction and joinery and in the manufacture of fibreboard and paper.

Softwood boards
Whole boards of home-grown timber, complete with waney edge and bark, can be bought from local sawmills. The 'waney edge' is the uncut edge of the board. Imported boards are usually supplied debarked or square-edged. The larch example shows the bark, sapwood and mature heartwood. The sapwood is the light-coloured wood which is less resistant to fungal and insect attack than the heartwood.

Abies alba
SILVER FIR

Other names: Whitewood.

Sources: Central and Southern Europe.

Characteristics of the tree: A thin, straight-growing tree, about 40m (130ft) in height and 1m (3ft 3in) in diameter. It loses its lower branches as it grows.

Characteristics of the wood: A pale-cream, non-resinous and almost colourless wood, with straight grain and fine texture. Similar to and often marketed with Norway spruce (*Picea abies*). It can be knotty. It is not durable and would need preservative treatment for exterior use.

Workability: Easily worked with sharp hand and machine tools to produce a trouble-free smooth finish. It glues well.

Average dried weight: 480kg/m^3 (30lb/ft^3).

Finishing: Stains, paints and varnishes well.

Common uses: Joinery, building construction, boxes, plywood, poles.

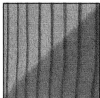

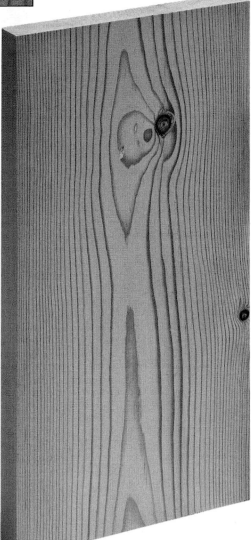

Agathis spp.
QUEENSLAND KAURI

Other names: North Queensland kauri, South Queensland kauri.

Sources: Australia.

Characteristics of the tree: A medium to large tree, reaching more than 45m (150ft) in height and 1.5m (5ft) in diameter. However, large trees are scarce due to overcutting.

Characteristics of the wood: A straight-grained wood, with fine even texture and lustrous surface. Colour varies from pale cream-brown to pinkish-brown. It is not a durable wood.

Workability: Works readily with hand and machine tools, and can be brought to a fine smooth finish.

Average dried weight: $480kg/m^3$ ($30lb/ft^3$).

Finishing: Takes stain and paint well, and can be polished to an excellent finish.

Common uses: Joinery, furniture.

Araucaria angustifolia
PARANA PINE

Other names: Brazilian pine (USA).

Sources: Argentina, Brazil and Paraguay.

Characteristics of the tree: A medium-size tree, reaching about 36m (120ft) in height, it has a long straight trunk with a flat crown of foliage at the top. The trunk can reach 1m (3ft 3in) in diameter.

Characteristics of the wood: Even-textured straight-grained timber, with inconspicuous growth rings. Light-brown heartwood, with dark-brown core. Often flecked with bright-red streaks. It produces large knot-free boards, but tends to buckle if not well seasoned. It is not a durable wood.

Workability: Easy to cut and shape with hand and machine tools, and can be brought to a smooth finish. It glues well.

Average dried weight: 540kg/m^3 (33lb/ft^3).

Finishing: Accepts stain, paint and polishes well.

Common uses: Joinery, furniture, turnery, plywood.

Araucaria cunninghamii
HOOP PINE

Other names: Queensland pine (though not a true pine).

Sources: Australia, Papua New Guinea.

Characteristics of the tree: A tall, elegant tree, with tufts of foliage at the tips of its thin branches. The average height is about 30m (100ft), with a trunk diameter of about 1m (3ft 3in).

Characteristics of the wood: A straight-grained fine-textured wood. Similar to Parana pine in appearance, it has wide light-brown sapwood with yellow-brown heartwood. It is not durable.

Workability: Works well with hand and machine tools, but requires a keen cutting edge to avoid tearing the grain around fine knots. It glues well.

Average dried weight: 560kg/m^3 (35lb/ft^3).

Finishing: Takes paint well and can be polished to a fine attractive finish.

Common uses: Joinery, furniture, turnery, building construction, pattern-making, plywood.

25

Cedrus libani
CEDAR OF LEBANON

Other names: True cedar.

Sources: Middle East.

Characteristics of the tree: A large tree, reaching about 40m (130ft) in height and approximately 1.5m (5ft) in diameter. Parkland-grown trees have a broad crown, with large low-spreading branches.

Characteristics of the wood: An aromatic wood, with light-brown heartwood of medium-fine texture. Clearly marked grain produced by contrasting earlywood and latewood. It can be knotty. It is a durable wood.

Workability: The straight-grained soft but brittle wood works easily with hand and machine tools, but can be difficult around knots. It sands well.

Average dried weight: 560kg/m³ (35lb/ft³).

Finishing: The wood takes paint and polishes well, and can be brought to a very fine finish.

Common uses: Interior and garden furniture, joinery, building construction.

Chamaecyparis nootkatensis
YELLOW CEDAR

Other names: Alaska yellow cedar, Pacific coast yellow cedar.

Sources: Pacific coast of North America.

Characteristics of the tree: A slow-growing, elegant, conically shaped tree of moderate size, reaching 30m (100ft) in height and 1m (3ft 3in) in diameter.

Characteristics of the wood: A pale-yellow even-textured wood, with fine straight grain. It is relatively light, stiff and stable when dry. It has excellent strength and wear properties and resistance to decay.

Workability: Can be worked easily with hand and machine tools. Good-quality wood can be cut to fine tolerances. It glues well.

Average dried weight: 500kg/m³ (31lb/ft³).

Finishing: Takes stain, polishes and paint well, and can be brought to a fine finish.

Common uses: Furniture, high-class joinery (including doors, windows, decorative panelling, mouldings and flooring), boatbuilding, oars, paddles, veneer.

Dacrydium cupressinum
RIMU

Other names: Red pine.

Sources: New Zealand.

Characteristics of the tree: A tall, straight-growing tree, it can reach 36m (120ft) in height and produces a long, clean, straight trunk up to 2.5m (8ft) in diameter.

Characteristics of the wood: A fine even-textured straight-grained timber. The heartwood is reddish brown, turning to lighter shades of brown through to the pale-yellow sapwood. It has a rather indistinct figure, with patches and streaks of browns and yellows blending together. The wood will lighten in colour on exposure to light.

Workability: Works well with hand and machine tools. Its fine texture gives a good finish from the plane and can be brought to a smooth finish. It glues satisfactorily.

Average dried weight: 530kg/m³ (33lb/ft³).

Finishing: Can be stained satisfactorily, and finishes well with paint or polish.

Common uses: Furniture, panelling, plywood, decorative veneer, turnery.

Larix decidua
LARCH

Other names: None.

Sources: Europe, particularly mountainous areas.

Characteristics of the tree: The tree grows to an approximate height of 45m (150ft) and produces a straight cylindrical trunk with a diameter of around 1m (3ft 3in). Larches shed their needles in winter.

Characteristics of the wood: Tougher than most softwoods, it is a straight-grained resinous timber of uniform texture, but can contain hard knots that loosen after seasoning. Heartwood is orange-red in colour, with narrow light-coloured sapwood. It is a relatively durable wood for exterior use.

Workability: Can be worked relatively easily with hand and machine tools, but knots can blunt cutting edges.

Average dried weight: 590kg/m³ (37lb/ft³).

Finishing: Sands well, though the harder latewood grain may be left proud of the surface. It takes paint and varnish satisfactorily.

Common uses: Joinery (including door and window frames, flooring and staircases), pit props, boat planking, posts, fencing.

29

Picea abies
NORWAY SPRUCE

Other names: European whitewood, European spruce.

Sources: Europe.

Characteristics of the tree: An important timber-producing tree, it reaches an average height of about 36m (120ft) but can grow to 60m (200ft) in favourable conditions. Young trees are cultivated to provide the traditional Christmas tree.

Characteristics of the wood: A lustrous straight-grained even-textured wood, with almost white earlywood and pale yellow-brown latewood. The sapwood is virtually indistinguishable from the heartwood. It has similar strength properties to European redwood (*Pinus sylvestris*), but the growth rings are not so prominent. It is not a durable wood for exterior use.

Workability: An easy wood to work using hand and machine tools, it cuts cleanly and can be sanded to a fine surface. It glues well.

Average dried weight: 470kg/m³ (29lb/ft³).

Finishing: It can be sanded satisfactorily, and finishes well with paint and varnish.

Common uses: Interior building construction, joinery, flooring, boxes and plywood. Selected slow-grown wood has excellent tonal qualities, and is used for piano soundboards and violin and guitar bellies.

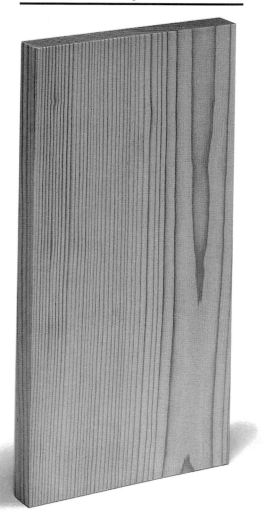

Picea sitchensis
SITKA SPRUCE

Other names: Silver spruce.

Sources: Canada, USA, UK.

Characteristics of the tree: A magnificent and important timber-producing tree that is fast-growing and widely cultivated in forests. It reaches a height of up to 87m (290ft), with a buttressed trunk of up to 5m (16ft) in diameter. However, forest-grown trees are generally of a smaller size.

Characteristics of the wood: A non-resinous, non-tainting creamy-white wood, with slightly pink heartwood. Usually straight-grained with even texture, depending on the rate of growth. It is relatively light and strong, with good elasticity, and can be steam-bent. It was used in the construction of the World War II 'Mosquito' aircraft.

Workability: Easy to work with hand and machine tools. However, it requires sharp cutting edges to avoid tearing the bands of earlywood on fast-grown species.

Average dried weight: 450kg/m^3 (28lb/ft^3).

Finishing: It stains well, and can be finished satisfactorily with paint and varnish.

Common uses: Boatbuilding, interior joinery, building construction, musical instruments, gliders, oars, racing sculls, plywood.

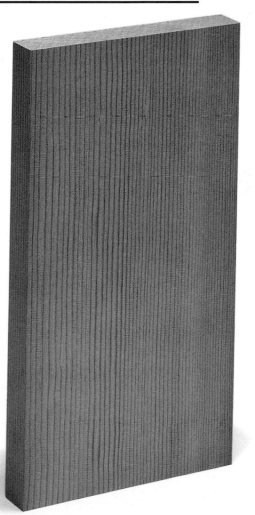

31

Pinus lambertiana
SUGAR PINE

Other names: Californian sugar pine.

Sources: USA.

Characteristics of the tree: Typically about 45m (150ft) in height and 1m (3ft 3in) in diameter, but can be more.

Characteristics of the wood: Moderately soft, with medium-coarse texture and even grain. It has white sapwood and pale-brown to reddish-brown heartwood. It is not durable.

Workability: Works well with hand and machine tools, but cutting edges must be kept sharp to avoid tearing the soft wood. It glues well.

Average dried weight: 430kg/m³ (26lb/ft³).

Finishing: Can be finished satisfactorily with stain, paint, varnish and polish.

Common uses: Joinery (such as doors, windows and mouldings), light building construction.

Pinus monticola
WESTERN WHITE PINE

Other names: Idaho white pine.

Sources: Canada, USA.

Characteristics of the tree: A medium-size tree, up to 37m (125ft) in height but can be taller. It produces a straight trunk about 1m (3ft 3in) in diameter.

Characteristics of the wood: A straight-grained even-textured wood. Pale yellow to reddish brown, with little variation in colour between earlywood and latewood. It has fine resin-duct lines, and is similar to but tougher than yellow pine (*Pinus strobus*, also known as white pine). It shrinks slightly more than yellow pine.

Workability: Works easily with hand and machine tools. It glues well.

Average dried weight: 450kg/m^3 (28lb/ft^3).

Finishing: It takes stain, paint and varnish well.

Common uses: Joinery (such as windows, doors and skirtings), building construction, built-in furniture, boatbuilding, pattern-making, plywood.

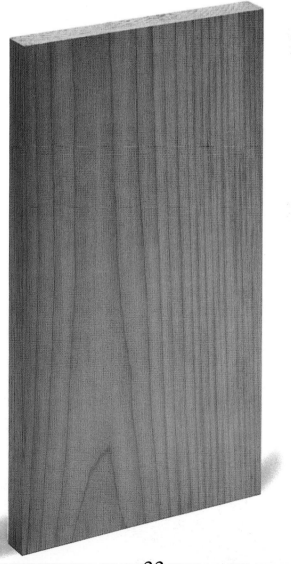

Pinus ponderosa
PONDEROSA PINE

Other names: Western yellow pine, Californian white pine (USA); British Columbia soft pine (Canada).

Sources: Western Canada and USA.

Characteristics of the tree: A medium to large tree which can reach 70m (230ft) in height. It has a straight trunk and an open conically shaped crown. A typical medium-sized tree produces a trunk about 750mm (2ft 6in) in diameter.

Characteristics of the wood: The wide pale-yellow sapwood is soft, non-resinous and even-textured. The heavier heartwood is deep yellow to reddish brown, and is resinous. It can be knotty, with resin ducts that show as fine dark lines on the surfaces of a board. It is not a durable wood.

Workability: Works well with hand and machine tools, although knots can be difficult, particularly when planing. It glues well.

Average dried weight: 480kg/m^3 (30lb/ft^3).

Finishing: It takes paint and varnish satisfactorily, but resinous wood should be treated with a sealer.

Common uses: Pattern-making, turnery, doors, furniture (sapwood); joinery, building construction (heartwood).

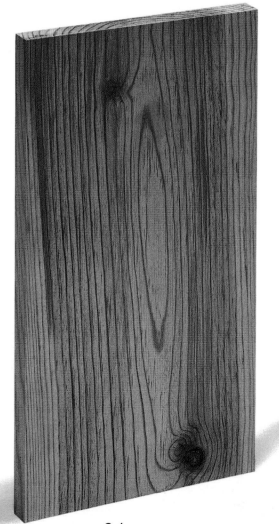

Pinus strobus
YELLOW PINE

Other names: Eastern white pine, northern white pine (USA); Quebec pine, Weymouth pine (UK).

Sources: USA, Eastern Canada.

Characteristics of the tree: A medium-size tree, about 30m (100ft) in height and up to 1m (3ft 3in) in diameter.

Characteristics of the wood: A soft and weak pine, with straight grain, fine even texture and inconspicuous annual growth rings. It is pale yellow to pale brown in colour, with fine resin-duct marks. It is noted for its low shrinkage and stability, but it is not durable.

Workability: Works easily with hand and machine tools, which must be kept sharp for best results. It is a good wood to carve, and glues well.

Average dried weight: 420kg/m³ (26lb/ft³).

Finishing: It takes stain, paint, varnish and polishes well.

Common uses: Engineering pattern-making, drawing boards, high-class joinery, furniture, light building construction, carving.

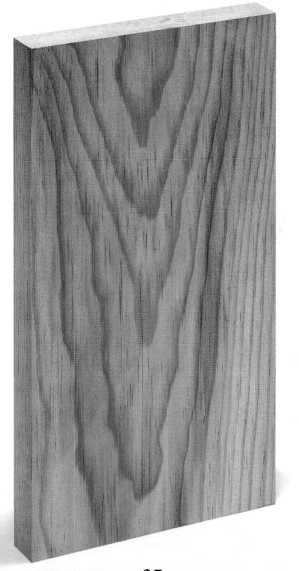

Pinus sylvestris
EUROPEAN REDWOOD

Other names: Scots pine, Scandinavian redwood, Russian redwood.

Sources: Europe, Northern Asia.

Characteristics of the tree: A medium-size tree, up to 30m (100ft) in height and 1m (3ft 3in) in diameter. An important timber-producing tree, it is conical in shape when young but becomes flat-topped with age.

Characteristics of the wood: A light-coloured resinous wood, with yellow-brown to reddish-brown heartwood (from which it gets its name) and light white-yellow sapwood. Distinct figure, with light earlywood and reddish latewood. It is stable in use and is a strong softwood, but not durable unless treated. Its light colour mellows with age.

Workability: Works well with hand and machine tools, but the presence of knots and resin can cause cutting and finishing problems. It glues well.

Average dried weight: 510kg/m³ (32lb/ft³).

Finishing: Stains satisfactorily, but the latewood can be more resistant and resinous pieces can be a problem. It accepts paint and varnish well, and can be brought to a good finish with polish.

Common uses: Building construction, interior joinery, furniture (selected knot-free timber), turnery, plywood.

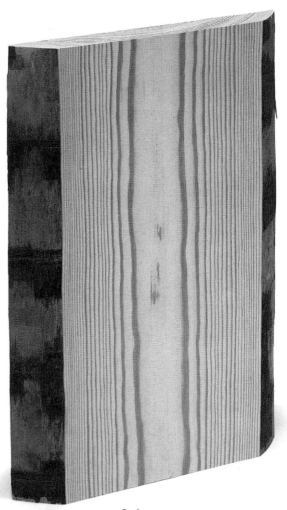

Pseudotsuga menziesii
DOUGLAS FIR

Other names: British Columbian pine, Oregon pine.

Sources: Canada, Western USA, UK.

Characteristics of the tree: A tall tree with a straight trunk, it grows to an average height of about 60m (200ft) but can reach 90m (300ft). Forest-grown trees produce trunks up to 2m (6ft 6in) in diameter and are free of branches for much of their height.

Characteristics of the wood: A straight-grained reddish-brown timber, with distinctive earlywood and latewood grain. Obtainable in large knot-free sizes.

Workability: Works well with hand and machine tools, but can dull cutting edges, which must be kept sharp. Can be brought to a smooth finish, but the harder latewood grain can be left proud of the surface after sanding.

Average dried weight: 530kg/m³ (33lb/ft³).

Finishing: Stains relatively well, although latewood is more resistant. It can be satisfactorily finished with paint and varnish.

Common uses: Joinery, plywood. Widely used in North America for building construction.

Sequoia sempervirens
SEQUOIA

Other names: Californian redwood.

Sources: USA.

Characteristics of the tree: A magnificent straight-growing tree, with short drooping branches. It grows to about 100m (330ft) in height, and its buttressed trunk can be more than 4.5m (15ft) in diameter. It has a distinctive red-coloured fissured bark, which can be more than 300mm (1ft) thick.

Characteristics of the wood: A straight-grained reddish-brown timber, with marked contrast between the earlywood and latewood. It is relatively soft, and the texture can vary from fine and even to relatively coarse. It is durable and suitable for exterior use.

Workability: Works well with hand and machine tools, but requires sharp cutting edges to prevent break-out along the cut. It glues and sands well.

Average dried weight: 420kg/m³ (26lb/ft³).

Finishing: Accepts paint well and can be brought to a good finish with polish.

Common uses: Shingles, exterior cladding, interior joinery, coffins, posts, plywood.

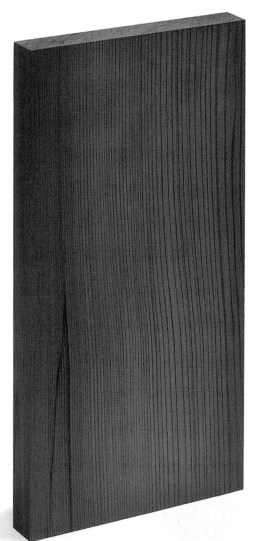

Taxus baccata
YEW

Other names: Common yew, European yew.

Sources: Europe, Asia Minor, North Africa, Burma and the Himalayas.

Characteristics of the tree: A relatively short tree, with a dense crown of evergreen foliage, it reaches an average height of about 15m (50ft). The trunk is short and deeply fluted where shoots have intergrown to produce an irregular form. Yews are the longest-living trees in Europe, with individual examples exceeding 1,000 years.

Characteristics of the wood: A tough, hard and durable softwood. It has an orange-red heartwood, with distinct light-coloured sapwood. The growth of the trunk produces irregular-shaped boards, often with holes, sapwood and bark inclusions. Small knots are common, but generally the growth pattern makes the wood very decorative. It has good bending properties and can be steam-bent.

Workability: Moderate to difficult, depending on the grain. Straight-grained wood can be worked and machined to a smooth finish, but the surface of irregular-grained wood can tear. It is an excellent wood for turning.

Average dried weight: 670kg/m^3 (42lb/ft^3).

Finishing: It accepts stain satisfactorily and polishes to an excellent finish.

Common uses: Furniture, turnery, carving, interior joinery, veneer.

39

Thuja plicata
WESTERN RED CEDAR

Other names: Giant arbor vitae (USA); red cedar (Canada); British Columbia red cedar (UK).

Sources: Canada, USA, UK, New Zealand.

Characteristics of the tree: A large conically shaped tree with dense foliage, it reaches a height of up to 75m (250ft) and a diameter of up to 2.5m (8ft).

Characteristics of the wood: A non-resinous relatively soft but durable aromatic timber, with straight grain and coarse texture. Reddish brown in colour, fading to silver-grey after long exposure to weathering. Attacks ferrous metals causing black stains.

Workability: Although soft and brittle, it is easily worked with hand and machine tools. It splits easily along the grain – a technique used to produce natural-looking roof shingles. It glues well.

Average dried weight: 370kg/m³ (23lb/ft³).

Finishing: It takes stain and paint well, and can be brought to a good finish.

Common uses: Doors and windows, shingles, exterior boarding, cladding and decking, greenhouses and sheds, fences, garden furniture and interior panelling.

Tsuga heterophylla
WESTERN HEMLOCK

Other names: Pacific hemlock, British Columbian hemlock.

Sources: Canada, USA, UK.

Characteristics of the tree: A tall, straight, elegant tree, with distinctive drooping top, it reaches 60m (200ft) in height and 2m (6ft 6in) in diameter. It produces large pieces of knot-free timber.

Characteristics of the wood: A pale-brown semi-lustrous wood, with relatively distinct growth rings. It is even-textured, has straight grain, and is non-resinous. It is not a durable wood and must be treated for exterior use.

Workability: Works well with hand and machine tools. It glues well.

Average dried weight: 500kg/m^3 (31lb/ft^3).

Finishing: Accepts stain, paint, varnish and polishes well.

Common uses: Building construction (often used in place of Douglas fir), joinery, plywood.

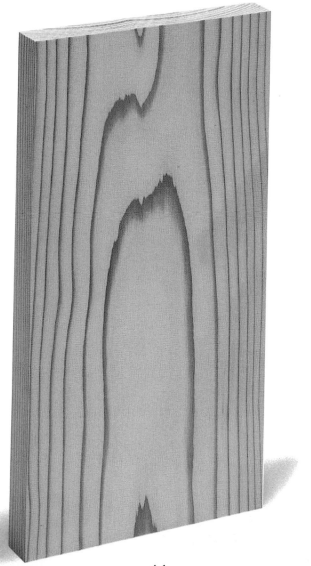

TREE CONSERVATION

The conservation of trees is an issue of great importance to everyone, not just wood users. Trees are a natural resource that provides important raw materials widely used in the making of our surroundings. They also play a key role in controlling our environment.

Controlling carbon dioxide

Carbon dioxide is a constituent of the earth's atmosphere and is a by-product of burning fossil fuels. Trees absorb carbon dioxide and help to maintain the natural balance of the earth's atmosphere. However, the level of carbon dioxide is rising faster than can be naturally absorbed. With other gases, it is producing the 'greenhouse effect', trapping the earth's radiated heat and causing global warming.

The deliberate burning of Amazonian rainforests, to clear land for crops or cattle, is not only reducing the stock of virgin forest but is also contributing to the greenhouse effect. In the northern hemisphere, the polluted air is producing acid rain that is causing many trees to die.

Alternative sources of energy and efficient energy conservation must therefore be developed, and emissions of carbon dioxide and other pollutants controlled.

Tropical hardwoods

Even with new materials and technologies, wood continues to be used in all manner of ways at an ever increasing rate. Such is the demand for tropical hardwoods that some species are near extinction.

Concerned conservationists have called for a complete ban on importing tropical hardwoods. While this could bring about the desired results, it would ־ have damaging repercussions for the timber trade and deprive developing countries of revenue. Logging is not the only cause. It is estimated that more timber is destroyed by burning than is exported. Mining operations, dam projects and stripping virgin forest for monoculture re-afforestation for the pulping industry also contribute to the problem.

Renewable resource

Trees are a renewable resource, and with sustainable management programmes it is possible to ensure the continued supply of tropical hardwoods.

As individual wood users, you can influence the timber trade by only using tropical hardwoods known to come from sustainable sources. Let your supplier know you are aware of the problem, and ask for assurances that the sources are well managed. If not, buy your wood elsewhere. Some retailers are now labelling their products to provide a consumer guide.

Using alternatives

The timbers of the temperate forests of North America and Europe are already produced by sustainable methods. More use must therefore be made of these woods as an alternative to tropical species. The chart on page 98 suggests alternatives for particular uses.

Temperate hardwoods may not offer such a wide choice of colour as 'exotic' tropical species, but you can use wood stain to good effect if required.

Endangered species

Temperate and tropical hardwoods are illustrated on the following pages. The tropical species most at risk are marked with a felled-tree symbol.

42

The term hardwood (like softwood) refers to the botanical grouping of the wood rather than its physical properties. It is, however, a useful label since the majority of hardwoods are in fact harder than woods from the softwood group. The outstanding exception is balsawood – which, although botanically a hardwood, is the softest wood in the two groups. Hardwoods come from broadleaved trees, which belong to the botanical group Angiospermae (flowering plants). Angiosperms produce seed-bearing ovaries that develop after fertilization into fruits or nuts. This group is regarded as a higher evolutionary order than the older and more primitive coniferous Gymnosperms, which have a simpler cell structure. Most broadleaved trees grown in temperate zones are deciduous and lose their leaves in winter – but not all, for some have developed into evergreens. Broadleaved trees grown in tropical forests are mainly evergreen. Hardwoods are generally more durable than softwoods and offer a wider choice of colour, texture and figure. They are also more expensive and many of them, particularly the highly prized exotic woods, are converted into veneer.

Distribution of hardwoods

- ■ Broadleaved evergreen forest
- ■ Broadleaved deciduous forest
- ■ Broadleaved evergreen and deciduous hardwood forest
- ■ Broadleaved deciduous and coniferous mixed forest

Hardwood regions of the world

There are thousands of species of hardwood trees distributed throughout the world, hundreds of which are harvested for commercial use. Climate is the most important factor governing which species grows where. In general, deciduous broadleaved trees are native to the temperate northern hemisphere and broadleaved evergreens to the tropics and southern hemisphere.

Hardwoods grow relatively slowly, and, although programmes for replanting help maintain the forests, the new trees are not always of such good quality as the older stock.

The map shows the distribution of broadleaved evergreens and broadleaved deciduous trees, evergreen and deciduous hardwoods, and broadleaved and coniferous mixed forests.

Acacia melanoxylon
AUSTRALIAN BLACKWOOD

Other names: Black wattle.

Sources: Mountainous regions of South and Eastern Australia.

Characteristics of the tree: A tree of moderate height, reaching 24m (80ft), with an average trunk diameter of about 1.5m (5ft).

Characteristics of the wood: Medium and even texture, with lustrous golden-brown to dark-brown colour. Generally straight-grained, but can be interlocked and wavy. Selected wavy-grain wood produces attractive fiddleback figure. It is a strong wood, with good bending properties. The heartwood is naturally durable and resistant to preservative treatment.

Workability: The wood works reasonably well with hand and machine tools. Straight-grained wood can be brought to a fine finish, but irregular grain can be difficult. It glues satisfactorily.

Average dried weight: 670kg/m^3 (41lb/ft^3).

Finishing: It stains well and produces a fine finish when polished.

Common uses: Fine furniture, high-class interior fittings, joinery, turnery, decorative veneer.

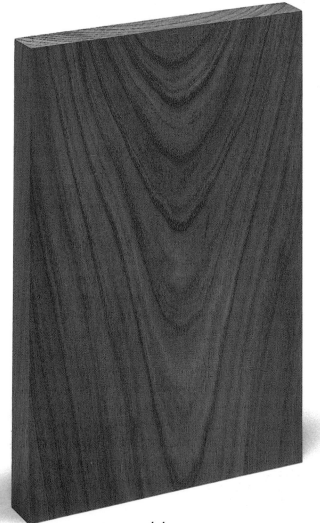

Acer pseudoplatanus
EUROPEAN SYCAMORE

Other names: Sycamore plane, great maple (UK); plane (Scotland).

Sources: Europe, Western Asia.

Characteristics of the tree: The tree can reach a height of 30m (100ft) and a diameter of 1.5m (5ft).

Characteristics of the wood: A fine even-textured wood – usually straight-grained, but can be wavy, producing fiddleback figure when quarter-sawn. It is white to yellowish white in colour, with a lustrous surface. A good wood for steam bending. It is not suitable for exterior use.

Workability: It works well with hand and machine tools, but wavy-grained wood needs care. It glues well.

Average dried weight: 630kg/m^3 (39lb/ft^3).

Finishing: It stains well and polishes to a fine finish.

Common uses: Turnery, furniture, kitchen utensils, flooring, veneer. Fiddleback sycamore is used for violin backs, from which it gets its name.

Acer rubrum
SOFT MAPLE

Other names: Red maple.

Sources: Canada, USA.

Characteristics of the tree: A tree of medium size, reaching 23m (75ft) in height and producing a trunk up to 750mm (2ft 6in) in diameter.

Characteristics of the wood: A straight-grained fine-textured wood, it is not as hard and strong as hard maple. The wood is lustrous and light creamy brown in colour. It has good steam-bending properties. Not naturally durable for outdoor use.

Workability: The wood works readily with hand and machine tools. It glues satisfactorily.

Average dried weight: 630kg/m³ (39lb/ft³).

Finishing: It stains well and polishes to a fine finish.

Common uses: Furniture, interior joinery, turnery, musical instruments, flooring, plywood, veneer.

46

Acer saccharum
HARD MAPLE

Other names: Rock maple, sugar maple.

Sources: Canada, USA.

Characteristics of the tree: A tree of moderate size, usually reaching about 27m (90ft) in height, with a trunk diameter of 750mm (2ft 6in).

Characteristics of the wood: A hard, heavy, straight-grained wood, with fine texture. The sapwood is white and is selected for its light colour; the heartwood is a light reddish-brown. The wood is hard-wearing, but not naturally durable for exterior use.

Workability: A difficult wood to work with hand and machine tools, particularly when the grain is irregular. It glues satisfactorily.

Average dried weight: 740kg/m^3 (46lb/ft^3).

Finishing: It stains and polishes satisfactorily.

Common uses: Furniture, turnery, musical instruments, butcher's blocks, flooring, veneer.

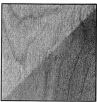

Alnus rubra
RED ALDER

Other names: Western alder, Oregon alder.

Sources: Pacific coast of North America.

Characteristics of the tree: A relatively small tree, reaching about 15m (50ft) in height and producing a trunk from 300 to 500mm (1ft to 1ft 8in) in diameter.

Characteristics of the wood: A soft relatively low-strength straight-grained even-textured wood, pale yellow to reddish brown in colour with a subtle figure. It is non-durable, but can be treated with preservative.

Workability: It works well with hand and machine tools, but sharp cutting edges need to be maintained to prevent tearing the grain. It glues well.

Average dried weight: 530kg/m^3 (33lb/ft^3).

Finishing: It takes stain well and can be brought to a good finish with paint or polish.

Common uses: Furniture, turnery, carving, toys, plywood, veneer.

Astronium fraxinifolium
GONÇALO ALVES

Other names: Zebrawood (UK); tigerwood (USA).

Sources: Brazil.

Characteristics of the tree: A tree of medium size, producing a straight trunk about 1m (3ft 3in) in diameter.

Characteristics of the wood: A hard medium-textured wood, with irregular interlocked grain and hard and soft layers of material. It is reddish brown in colour with dark brown streaks, and is similar in appearance to rosewood. The wood is naturally very durable.

Workability: A difficult wood to work, requiring regular sharpening of the tools. It is a good wood for turning and glues well.

Average dried weight: 950kg/m^3 (59lb/ft^3).

Finishing: The wood finishes with a natural lustre and polishes to a fine finish.

Common uses: Fine furniture, turnery, decorative woodware, veneer.

49

Betula alleghaniensis
YELLOW BIRCH

Other names: Hard birch, betula wood (Canada); Canadian yellow birch, Quebec birch, American birch (UK).

Sources: Canada, USA.

Characteristics of the tree: The largest of the North American birches, the tree usually reaches about 20m (65ft) in height. Its straight, slightly tapering trunk is generally about 750mm (2ft 6in) in diameter, but can be more, depending on growing conditions.

Characteristics of the wood: A straight-grained wood, with fine even texture. It has light-yellow sapwood, and reddish-brown heartwood with distinct darker-coloured growth rings. It has good steam-bending properties. It is not durable and the heartwood is resistant to preservative treatment. The sapwood is permeable.

Workability: It works reasonably well with hand tools, and machines and glues well.

Average dried weight: 710kg/m³ (44lb/ft³).

Finishing: It stains well and can be polished to a fine light-coloured finish.

Common uses: Furniture, joinery, flooring, turnery, high-grade plywood.

Betula papyrifera
PAPER BIRCH

Other names: American birch (UK); white birch (Canada).

Sources: Canada, USA.

Characteristics of the tree: A relatively small tree, on average about 18m (60ft) in height. The straight, clear, cylindrical trunk is usually about 300mm (1ft) in diameter, but can be larger.

Characteristics of the wood: A fine straight-grained even-textured wood. It has a wide creamy-white sapwood and pale-brown heartwood. The wood is fairly hard and has moderate steam-bending properties. It is not durable and the heartwood is relatively resistant to preservative treatment.

Workability: It works reasonably well with hand and machine tools, and glues well.

Average dried weight: 640kg/m³ (40lb/ft³).

Finishing: It stains well and can be polished to a fine finish like yellow birch.

Common uses: Turnery, domestic woodware, plywood, veneer, crates.

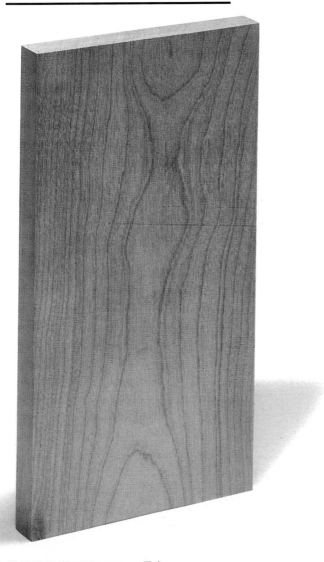

51

Buxus sempervirens
BOXWOOD

Other names: European, Turkish, Iranian boxwood (according to origin).

Sources: Southern Europe, Asia Minor, Western Asia

Characteristics of the tree: A small shrublike tree, reaching not more than 9m (30ft) in height. It produces short lengths or billets, usually not more than 1m (3ft 3in) in length and up to 200mm (8in) in diameter.

Characteristics of the wood: A very fine, even-textured wood. It is hard, dense and heavy, and can have straight or irregular grain. Pale yellow in colour when cut, it mellows on exposure. It is a tough wood and has good bending properties.

Workability: A hard wood to work, but cuts very cleanly with sharp tools. It is an excellent wood for turning on a lathe. It glues readily.

Average dried weight: 930kg/m³ (58lb/ft³).

Finishing: It stains well and polishes to a fine finish.

Common uses: Carving, turnery, tool handles, engraving blocks, musical-instrument parts, rulers, inlay.

Cardwellia sublimis
SILKY OAK

Other names: Northern silky oak (Australia); bull oak, Australian silky oak (UK).

Sources: Australia.

Characteristics of the tree: The tree reaches a height of around 36m (120ft) and produces a straight trunk up to 1.2m (4ft) in diameter.

Characteristics of the wood: A coarse even-textured wood, usually straight-grained with large rays giving an attractive ray figure. It is reddish brown in colour, similar to American red oak, although it is not a true oak. The wood has only moderate strength, but is good for steam bending. It is moderately durable for exterior use.

Workability: It works well with hand and machine tools, but the ray cells can tear when planing. It glues satisfactorily.

Average dried weight: 550kg/m^3 (34lb/ft^3).

Finishing: It stains well and polishes satisfactorily.

Common uses: Furniture, interior joinery, flooring, building construction, veneer.

Carya illinoensis
PECAN HICKORY

Other names: Sweet pecan.

Sources: USA.

Characteristics of the tree: A nut-bearing tree of relatively large size, reaching 30m (100ft) in height and 1m (3ft 3in) in diameter.

Characteristics of the wood: A coarse-textured wood, generally straight-grained but can be irregular or wavy. The sapwood is white, and the heartwood reddish brown in colour. A ring-porous wood, it is similar in appearance to ash. It is a dense, tough, shock-resisting wood, a little heavier than ash, but can vary according to the rate of growth. It is not naturally durable.

Workability: Dense fast-grown wood can be difficult to work and will quickly dull the tools. It glues satisfactorily.

Average dried weight: 750kg/m^3 (46lb/ft^3).

Finishing: Although ring-porous, it can be brought to a smooth finish and stains and polishes well.

Common uses: Striking-tool handles, sports equipment, chairs and bentwood furniture.

54

Castanea dentata
AMERICAN CHESTNUT

Other names: Wormy chestnut.

Sources: Canada, USA.

Characteristics of the tree: A tree of moderate size, usually about 24m (80ft) in height, producing a trunk 500mm (1ft 8in) in diameter. Once plentiful, supplies were severely reduced by a fungal disease called chestnut blight. Many trees were felled in an attempt to control the spread of the disease.

Characteristics of the wood: Coarse-textured, with wide prominent growth rings, it is similar to oak in appearance but lacks the oak's ray figure when quarter-sawn. It is also lighter in weight than oak. The heartwood is light brown in colour. Insect attack causes 'wormy chestnut', which is sought after for making 'period' furniture. It is a naturally durable wood.

Workability: An easy wood to work with hand and machine tools. It glues well.

Average dried weight: 480kg/m^3 (30lb/ft^3).

Finishing: It takes stain well and polishes to a fine finish.

Common uses: Furniture, coffins, poles, stakes, decorative veneer.

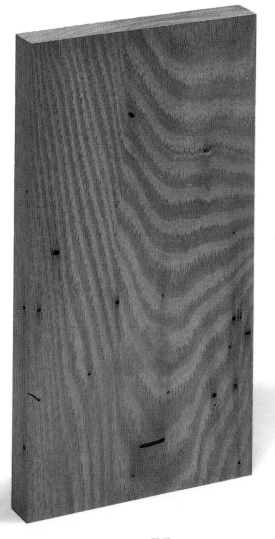

Castanea sativa
SWEET CHESTNUT

Other names: Spanish chestnut, European chestnut.

Sources: Europe, Asia Minor.

Characteristics of the tree: Known for its edible nuts, it is a moderate to large tree some 30m (100ft) or more in height. It produces a straight trunk, 6m (20ft) long and about 1.8m (6ft) in diameter.

Characteristics of the wood: A coarse-textured wood, yellowish brown in colour, with straight or spiralled grain. The colour and texture is similar to oak when plain-sawn, but it does not display the ray figure of oak when quarter-sawn. Like oak, chestnut will corrode ferrous metals and become stained when in contact with them. The wood is naturally durable.

Workability: An easy wood to work and finish with hand and machine tools. It glues well.

Average dried weight: 560kg/m³ (35lb/ft³).

Finishing: Although coarse-textured, it can be brought to a smooth finish. It stains well and gives an excellent finish with varnish and polish.

Common uses: Furniture, turnery, coffins, poles, stakes.

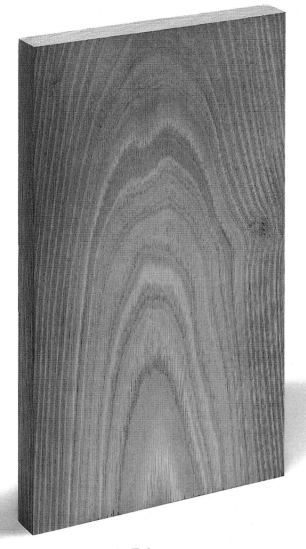

Castanospermum australe
BLACKBEAN

Other names: Moreton Bay bean, Moreton Bay chestnut, beantree.

Sources: Eastern Australia.

Characteristics of the tree: A tall tree found in moist forest regions from Queensland to New South Wales. It reaches about 40m (130ft) in height and produces a trunk about 1m (3ft 3in) or more in diameter.

Characteristics of the wood: A wood with attractive figure, it is rich brown in colour with grey-brown streaks. Generally a straight-grained wood, but it can be interlocked. It is hard and heavy, and is rather coarse in texture. The heartwood is naturally durable and resistant to preservative treatment.

Workability: Not a particularly easy wood to work with hand or machine tools. Although hard, the softer patches of the wood can crumble if cutting edges are not kept sharp. It glues reasonably well, but can vary.

Average dried weight: 720kg/m^3 (45lb/ft^3).

Finishing: It stains well and can be polished to a fine finish with the usual range of materials.

Common uses: Fine furniture, joinery, turnery, carving, decorative veneers.

Chloroxylon swietenia
SATINWOOD

Other names: East Indian satinwood.

Sources: Central and Southern India, Sri Lanka.

Characteristics of the tree: A relatively small tree, reaching about 15m (50ft) in height and producing a straight trunk about 300mm (1ft) in diameter.

Characteristics of the wood: A strong, hard and heavy lustrous wood, with fine even texture and interlocked grain that produces a striped figure. It is light yellow to golden brown in colour, with thin dark streaks. It is a naturally durable wood.

Workability: A moderately difficult wood to work with hand and machine tools, though it turns well. It is rather difficult to glue.

Average dried weight: 990kg/m³ (61lb/ft³).

Finishing: With care, it can be brought to a smooth surface and polished to a fine finish.

Common uses: Furniture, interior joinery, turnery, veneer, inlay bandings.

Dalbergia cearensis
KINGWOOD

Other names: Violet wood, violetta (USA).

Sources: South America.

Characteristics of the tree: A small tree, botanically related to rosewood, that produces short logs or billets of wood not usually exceeding 2.5m (8ft) in length. The diameter of the billets can be 75 to 200mm (3 to 8in) with the sapwood removed.

Characteristics of the wood: A fine even-textured, heavy, lustrous wood. It has a white sapwood, contrasting sharply with the dark heartwood, which has an attractive variegated striped figure of violet-brown, black and golden yellow.

Workability: The hard nature of the wood requires sharp tools, but otherwise it is relatively easy to work. It glues satisfactorily.

Average dried weight: 1200kg/m^3 (75lb/ft^3).

Finishing: It burnishes to a fine natural finish and polishes well with wax.

Common uses: Inlay, turnery, marquetry.

Dalbergia latifolia
INDIAN ROSEWOOD

Other names: East Indian rosewood, Bombay rosewood (UK); Bombay blackwood (India).

Sources: India.

Characteristics of the tree: Size varies according to growing conditions, but the tree can reach 24m (80ft) in height. It produces a straight, clear, cylindrical trunk up to 1.5m (5ft) in diameter.

Characteristics of the wood: A hard, heavy, moderately coarse wood, with uniform texture. It has a subtle ribbon-grain figure due to interlocked narrow bands. The colour is golden brown to purple-brown, with streaks of dark purple or black. It is a naturally durable wood.

Workability: It is moderately difficult to work with hand tools and has a dulling effect on cutting edges of machine tools. It glues satisfactorily.

Average dried weight: 870kg/m^3 (54lb/ft^3).

Finishing: The grain requires filling to achieve a high polish. It responds well to a wax finish.

Common uses: Furniture, shop fittings, musical instruments, boatbuilding, turnery, veneer.

Dalbergia nigra
BRAZILIAN ROSEWOOD

Other names: Rio rosewood, Bahia rosewood (UK); jacaranda da Bahia, jacaranda preto (Brazil); palissander, palissandre du Brazil (France).

Sources: Brazil.

Characteristics of the tree: A tall slender tree, it can grow to 37m (125ft) in height, with a trunk around 600mm (2ft) in diameter.

Characteristics of the wood: A beautiful, hard and heavy wood, with medium texture. Usually straight-grained, it is highly figured, with rich brown to violet-brown colour streaked with black markings. The wood is oily and gets its name from the slightly perfumed aroma it gives off. It is strong and steam-bends well. It is naturally durable.

Workability: Because of its hardness, it is relatively difficult to work with hand tools and quickly dulls the cutting edges of machine tools. Gluing is improved by the use of an oil solvent.

Average dried weight: 870kg/m³ (54lb/ft³).

Finishing: It can be burnished to a fine natural finish, oiled or polished.

Common uses: Furniture, joinery, turnery, carving, decorative veneer.

61

Dalbergia retusa
COCOBOLO

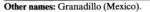

Other names: Granadillo (Mexico).

Sources: West coast of Central America.

Characteristics of the tree: A tree of moderate size, reaching 30m (100ft) in height and producing a fluted trunk about 1m (3ft 3in) in diameter.

Characteristics of the wood: Hard and heavy, it is a naturally durable wood with irregular grain and medium-fine uniform texture. The heartwood has an attractive variegated colour, from purple-red to yellow, with black markings. The colour turns to deep orange-red on exposure.

Workability: Although hard, it works readily with hand and machine tools provided they are kept sharp. The wood is slightly oily and machines to a fine smooth surface. It is difficult to glue.

Average dried weight: 1100kg/m³ (68lb/ft³).

Finishing: It can be stained and polished to a fine finish.

Common uses: Turnery, cutlery handles, brush backs, decorative veneer.

Diospyros ebenum
EBONY

Other names: Tendu, tuki, ebans.

Sources: Sri Lanka, India.

Characteristics of the tree: A relatively small tree, producing a straight trunk up to 4.5m (15ft) in height and 750mm (2ft 6in) in diameter.

Characteristics of the wood: A hard, dense and heavy wood, with a fine even texture and straight, irregular or wavy grain. The sapwood is yellowish white, the heartwood a lustrous dark brown to black. The heartwood is naturally durable.

Workability: A difficult wood to work by hand or machine. It chips easily and quickly dulls the tools. However, it can be machined well on a lathe and brought to a fine finish. It does not glue well.

Average dried weight: 1190kg/m^3 (74lb/ft^3).

Finishing: It can be polished to an excellent finish.

Common uses: Turnery, musical instruments, cutlery handles, inlay.

Endiandra palmerstonii
QUEENSLAND WALNUT

Other names: Australian walnut, walnut bean, oriental wood.

Sources: Australia.

Characteristics of the tree: A tall tree, reaching 42m (140ft) in height and producing a long buttressed trunk about 1.5m (5ft) in diameter.

Characteristics of the wood: Similar to European walnut in appearance, but not a true walnut. The wood usually has interlocked and wavy grain, producing an attractive figure. The colour can vary from light to dark brown, with pinkish to dark-greyish streaks. Silica is often present in the ray cells. It is non-durable and is not suitable for exterior use.

Workability: A difficult wood to work because of the dulling effect on cutting edges, but it can be brought to a smooth finish. It glues satisfactorily.

Average dried weight: 690kg/m³ (43lb/ft³).

Finishing: It polishes to a fine finish.

Common uses: Furniture, interior joinery, shop fittings, flooring, veneer.

Entandrophragma utile
UTILE

Other names: Sipo (Ivory Coast); assié (Cameroons).

Sources: Africa.

Characteristics of the tree: A large tree, some 45m (150ft) in height, producing a straight cylindrical trunk about 2m (6ft 6in) in diameter.

Characteristics of the wood: A medium-textured wood, usually with interlocked grain producing a ribbon-striped figure when quarter-sawn. It is pinkish brown in colour when freshly cut, turning reddish brown on exposure. It is a moderately strong wood and durable.

Workability: It works well with hand and machine tools, but the ribbon-striped figure can tear when planing. It glues well.

Average dried weight: 660kg/m³ (41lb/ft³).

Finishing: It stains and polishes well.

Common uses: Furniture, interior and exterior joinery, boatbuilding, flooring, plywood, veneer.

Eucalyptus marginata
JARRAH

Other names: None.

Sources: Western Australia.

Characteristics of the tree: A large tree reaching 45m (150ft) in height and producing a long clear trunk around 1.5m (5ft) in diameter.

Characteristics of the wood: A strong, hard and heavy wood, with an even medium-coarse texture. Usually straight-grained, but can be wavy or interlocked. It has a narrow yellowish-white sapwood and light to deep red-brown heartwood. The colour of unfinished wood, however, is likely to mellow to a lighter shade of brown. The figure displays fine brown flecks with occasional gum veins. Sometimes the wood is decoratively marked by the fungus *Fistulina hepatica*. It is naturally very durable.

Workability: A moderately difficult wood to work with hand and machine tools, but turns very well. It glues satisfactorily.

Average dried weight: 820kg/m^3 (51lb/ft^3).

Finishing: It polishes very well and is particularly suited to an oil finish.

Common uses: Marine construction, building construction, exterior and interior joinery, furniture, turnery, decorative veneers.

66

Fagus grandifolia
AMERICAN BEECH

Other names: None.

Sources: Canada, USA.

Characteristics of the tree: A relatively small tree, with an average height of 15m (50ft), it produces a trunk about 500mm (1ft 8in) in diameter.

Characteristics of the wood: A straight-grained wood, with fine even texture. Light brown to reddish brown in colour, it is slightly coarser and heavier than European beech (*Fagus sylvatica*), but has similar strength and bending properties. It will readily decay if exposed to moisture, but can be preservative-treated.

Workability: It can be worked well with hand tools and machines, but there is a tendency to scorch on crosscutting and drilling. It can be steam-bent successfully and glues well.

Average dried weight: 740kg/m³ (46lb/ft³).

Finishing: It stains well and can be polished to a fine finish with the usual range of materials.

Common uses: Cabinet-making, bentwood furniture, interior joinery, turnery.

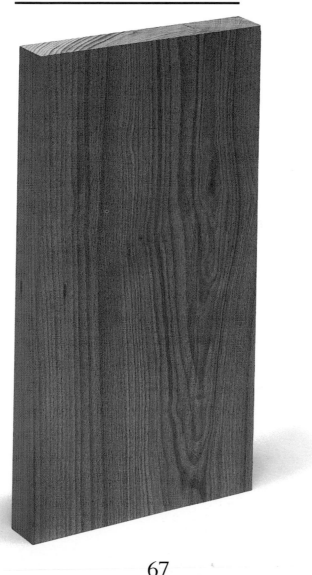

Fagus sylvatica
EUROPEAN BEECH

Other names: English, Danish, French beech etc. (according to origin).

Sources: Europe.

Characteristics of the tree: A large important timber-producing tree, some 45m (150ft) in height, with a straight clear trunk about 1.2m (4ft) in diameter.

Characteristics of the wood: A straight-grained wood, with fine even texture. Freshly cut it is whitish brown, turning yellowish brown on exposure. 'Steamed beech' (wood that has been steam-treated as part of the seasoning process) turns reddish brown. It is a strong wood, with excellent steam-bending properties, and is tougher than oak when seasoned. Beech is perishable, but can be preservative treated.

Workability: The ease of working depends on the quality of the wood and how well it is seasoned. It works readily with hand and machine tools, and can be brought to a fine finish. It glues well.

Average dried weight: 720kg/m^3 (45lb/ft^3).

Finishing: It stains well and can be polished to a fine finish with the usual range of materials.

Common uses: Cabinet-making, bentwood furniture, interior joinery, veneer, turnery, plywood.

Fraxinus americana
AMERICAN WHITE ASH

Other names: Canadian ash (UK); white ash (USA).

Sources: Canada and USA.

Characteristics of the tree: A small to medium-size tree, approximately 15 to 18m (50 to 60ft) in height, with a trunk about 750mm (2ft 6in) in diameter.

Characteristics of the wood: A coarse but generally straight-grained wood with almost white sapwood, and pale-brown heartwood similar to European ash. It is ring-porous, with a distinct figure. A strong tough wood, with good steam-bending and shock-resistant properties. It is non-durable, and not suited to outdoor use unless treated with a preservative.

Workability: Works well with hand and machine tools, and can be brought to a fine finish. It glues well.

Average dried weight: 670kg/m^3 (42lb/ft^3).

Finishing: It stains well (often finished in black) and also finishes well with polish.

Common uses: Sports equipment and tool handles, boatbuilding, joinery, plywood, decorative veneer.

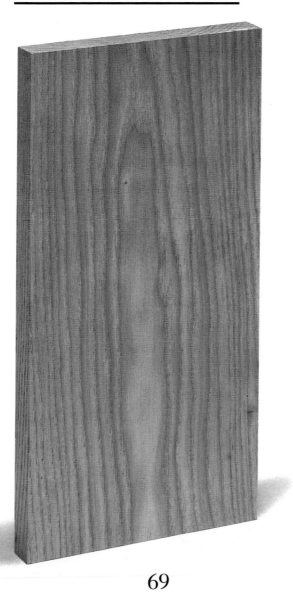

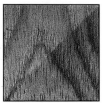

Fraxinus excelsior
EUROPEAN ASH

Other names: English, French, Polish ash etc. (according to origin).

Sources: Europe.

Characteristics of the tree: A tree of moderate to large size, some 30m (100ft) or more in height, producing a trunk from 500mm to 1.5m (1ft 8in to 5ft) in diameter.

Characteristics of the wood: A tough coarse-textured straight-grained wood, whitish to pale brown in colour, with little distinction between heartwood and sapwood. Logs with dark-stained heartwood produce 'olive ash'. An excellent wood for steam bending, it is also relatively resistant to shock and is widely used for tool handles and sports equipment. Selected material known as 'sports' ash is in high demand. The wood is perishable and is unsuitable for exterior use unless treated.

Workability: It works well with hand and machine tools, and glues well. Its flexible and split-resistant properties make it easy to bend.

Average dried weight: 710kg/m^3 (44lb/ft^3).

Finishing: Although coarse-textured, the wood can be brought to a smooth finish. It accepts stain well and can be finished with all types of polish.

Common uses: Sports equipment and tool handles, bentwood furniture, cabinet-making, vehicle bodies, ladder rungs, boatbuilding, laminated work, plywood, decorative veneer.

70

Gonystylus macrophyllum
RAMIN

Other names: Melawis (Malaysia); ramin telur (Sarawak).

Sources: Southeast Asia.

Characteristics of the tree: A tree of medium size, reaching about 24m (80ft) in height, with a long straight trunk about 600mm (2ft) in diameter.

Characteristics of the wood: A moderately fine even-textured wood, usually straight-grained but can be slightly interlocked. A rather plain wood, with pale creamy-brown heartwood and sapwood. It is a perishable wood, unsuited to exterior use.

Workability: It works reasonably well with hand and machine tools, but cutting across the grain can cause break-out if the cutting edges are not sharp. It glues well.

Average dried weight: 670kg/m^3 (41lb/ft^3).

Finishing: It takes stain, paint and varnish well, and polishes satisfactorily.

Common uses: Furniture, interior joinery, turnery, toys, carving, flooring, veneer.

Guaiacum officinale
LIGNUM VITAE

Other names: Guayacan (Spain); bois de gaiac (France); guayacan negro, pala santo (Cuba); ironwood (USA).

Sources: West Indies and tropical America.

Characteristics of the tree: A small slow-growing tree, reaching not more than 9m (30ft) in height and producing a trunk about 500mm (1ft 8in) in diameter. The wood is sold in short billets.

Characteristics of the wood: A very hard and heavy wood. It has a fine, uniform texture and closely interlocked grain. The heartwood is dark greenish brown to black and is in sharp contrast to the narrow cream-coloured sapwood. It is a resinous wood, with an oily feel. It is naturally very durable and known for its hardness and self-lubricating properties.

Workability: It is very difficult to saw and plane with hand and machine tools. It is an excellent wood for turning and can be brought to a fine finish. It does not glue well unless treated with an oil solvent.

Average dried weight: $1250kg/m^3$ ($78lb/ft^3$).

Finishing: It burnishes to a fine natural finish.

Common uses: Bearings, pulleys, mallets, turnery.

Guibourtia demeusei
BUBINGA

Other names: African rosewood; kevazingo (Gabon); essingang (Cameroons).

Sources: Cameroons, Gabon.

Characteristics of the tree: A tree of moderate size, reaching 30m (100ft) in height and producing a long straight trunk about 1m (3ft 3in) in diameter.

Characteristics of the wood: A moderately coarse even-textured wood. The heartwood is red-brown in colour, with red and purple veining. It is hard and heavy, with straight or interlocked and irregular grain. It is not resilient, but reasonably strong and durable.

Workability: It works well with hand tools, and machines to a fine finish. Irregular-grained wood can be difficult, and sharp cutting edges must be maintained. Gum pockets can give problems when gluing.

Average dried weight: 880kg/m³ (55lb/ft³).

Finishing: It stains well and polishes to a fine finish.

Common uses: Decorative veneer (called kevazingo when rotary cut), turnery, woodware, furniture.

Guilandina echinata
BRAZILWOOD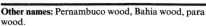

Other names: Pernambuco wood, Bahia wood, para wood.

Sources: Brazil.

Characteristics of the tree: A small to medium-size tree, producing short lengths or billets not more than 200mm (8in) in diameter.

Characteristics of the wood: Hard and heavy, generally with straight grain and fine even texture. It has pale sapwood, contrasting with the lustrous bright orange-red heartwood which turns to a rich red-brown on exposure. It is tough, resilient and very durable.

Workability: The wood works reasonably well with hand and machine tools, but requires regular maintenance of cutting edges. It glues well.

Average dried weight: 1280kg/m³ (80lb/ft³).

Finishing: It is naturally lustrous and polishes to a beautiful fine finish.

Common uses: Dyewood, turnery, violin bows, gun stocks, parquet flooring, exterior joinery, veneer.

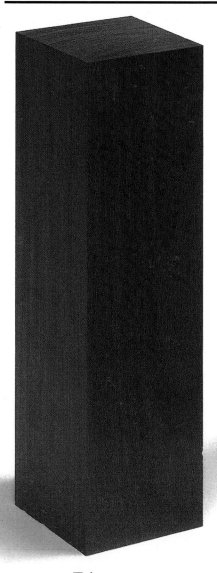

74

Juglans cinerea
BUTTERNUT

Other names: White walnut.

Sources: Canada, USA.

Characteristics of the tree: An American species of walnut, it is a relatively small tree, reaching about 15m (50ft) in height, with a trunk about 750mm (2ft 6in) in diameter depending on growing conditions.

Characteristics of the wood: A straight-grained coarse-textured wood with medium-brown to dark-brown heartwood, but not as dark as black walnut, which it generally resembles. It is a relatively soft weak wood and is not naturally durable.

Workability: It works easily with hand and machine tools, but requires sharp cutting edges as it is rather soft. It glues well.

Average dried weight: 450kg/m³ (28lb/ft³).

Finishing: It stains well and polishes to a fine finish.

Common uses: Furniture, carving, interior joinery, veneer, boxes, crates.

Juglans nigra
AMERICAN WALNUT

Other names: Black American walnut.

Sources: USA, Canada.

Characteristics of the tree: A moderate-size tree, reaching about 30m (100ft) and producing a trunk about 1.5m (5ft) in diameter.

Characteristics of the wood: A tough wood with even but rather coarse texture, usually straight-grained but can be wavy. The sapwood is light in colour, contrasting with the rich dark-brown to purplish-black heartwood. The wood is strong, moderately durable and has good steam-bending properties.

Workability: It works well with hand and machine tools and glues well.

Average dried weight: 660kg/m^3 (41lb/ft^3).

Finishing: It polishes to a fine finish.

Common uses: Furniture, gun stocks, interior joinery, musical instruments, turnery, carving, plywood, veneer.

Juglans regia
EUROPEAN WALNUT

Other names: English, French, Italian walnut etc. (according to origin).

Sources: Europe, Asia Minor, Southwest Asia.

Characteristics of the tree: A nut-bearing tree of moderate size, reaching about 30m (100ft) in height. The trunk is usually about 1m (3ft 3in) in diameter, but can be more.

Characteristics of the wood: A rather coarse-textured wood, with straight to wavy grain. typically grey-brown with darker streaks, though the colour and markings can vary according to origin. Italian walnut is generally considered the best for colour and figure. Walnut is a reasonably tough wood, with moderate durability and good steam-bending properties.

Workability: It works well with hand and machine tools, and glues satisfactorily.

Average dried weight: 670kg/m^3 (42lb/ft^3).

Finishing: It polishes to a fine finish.

Common uses: Furniture, interior joinery, gun stocks, turnery, carving, veneer.

77

Liriodendron tulipifera
AMERICAN WHITEWOOD

Other names: Yellow poplar, tulip poplar (USA); tulip tree (UK and USA); canary whitewood (UK).

Sources: Eastern USA, Canada.

Characteristics of the tree: The tree reaches 37m (125ft) in height and produces a trunk some 2m (6ft 6in) in diameter but can be more.

Characteristics of the wood: A moderately soft and lightweight wood, with straight grain and fine texture. The narrow sapwood is white; the heartwood pale-olive green to brown, with blue-coloured streaks. It is not a naturally durable wood and should not be used in contact with the ground.

Workability: It is an easy wood to use with hand and machine tools. It glues well.

Average dried weight: 510kg/m^3 (31lb/ft^3).

Finishing: It takes stain, paint, varnish and polishes well.

Common uses: Interior joinery, furniture, carving, light building construction, toys, plywood, veneer.

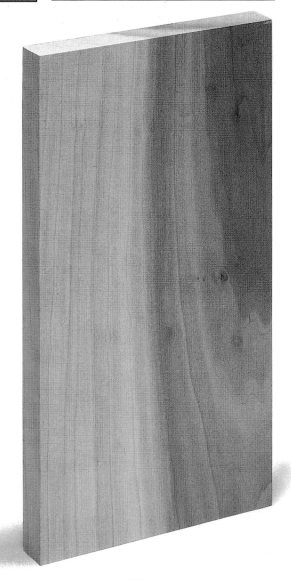

Ochroma lagopus
BALSA

Other names: Guano (Puerto Rico, Honduras); lanero (Cuba); polak (Belize, Nicaragua); topa (Peru); tami (Bolivia).

Sources: South America.

Characteristics of the tree: A fast-growing tree, reaching a height of some 21m (70ft) and a diameter of about 600mm (2ft) in 6 to 7 years. Thereafter the growth rate declines. It is not a long-lived tree, and reaches maturity in about 12 to 15 years.

Characteristics of the wood: The softest and lightest commercial hardwood. An open straight-grained lustrous wood, with very pale beige to pinkish colour. It is relatively strong for its weight and is graded on the basis of density. The fast-grown wood is lighter in weight than the denser, harder, slower-grown wood produced in later years. It is not a durable wood.

Workability: An easy wood to work with hand and machine tools, but it tends to crumble or tear if cutting edges are not sharp. It sands easily and glues well.

Average dried weight: 160kg/m^3 (10lb/ft^3).

Finishing: It is an absorbent wood which can be stained, painted and polished satisfactorily.

Common uses: Insulation, buoyancy aids, model-making, packaging for delicate items.

Peltogyne spp.
PURPLEHEART

Other names: Amaranth (USA); koroboreli, saka, sakavalli (Guyana); purperhart (Surinam); pau roxo, amarante (Brazil).

Sources: Central and South America.

Characteristics of the tree: A tall tree, producing a long straight trunk about 1m (3ft 3in) in diameter. The average height is 36m (120ft), but can be more.

Characteristics of the wood: A uniform wood, with fine to medium texture. It is usually straight-grained, but sometimes irregular. The wood displays an attractive purple colour when freshly cut, darkening to rich brown after a time due to oxidation. It is a strong, resilient wood and very durable.

Workability: It works moderately well, but quickly dulls cutting edges. The resin content makes machine cutting difficult. It is a good wood for turning, and glues well.

Average dried weight: 880kg/m^3 (55lb/ft^3).

Finishing: It takes stain, and finishes well with wax polish. Spirit-based polishes can affect the natural colour.

Common uses: Building construction, boatbuilding, flooring, furniture, turnery, veneer.

80

Pericopsis elata
AFRORMOSIA

Other names: Assemela (Ivory Coast, France); kokrodua (Ghana, Ivory Coast); ayin, egbi (Nigeria).

Sources: West Africa

Characteristics of the tree: A relatively tall tree, reaching a height of about 45m (150ft) and producing a long trunk about 1m (3ft 3in) in diameter.

Characteristics of the wood: A durable wood, with straight to interlocked grain. The yellow-brown heartwood darkens to the colour of teak, which it resembles, though it is finer textured and not so oily as teak. It is also stronger than teak. Afrormosia can react to ferrous metals in moist conditions, causing black stains.

Workability: It saws and planes well and can be brought to a smooth finish, but care is needed with interlocked grain. It glues well.

Average dried weight: 710kg/m^3 (44lb/ft^3).

Finishing: It can be polished to a fine finish.

Common uses: Veneer, interior and exterior joinery, interior and exterior furniture, building construction, boatbuilding.

Platanus acerifolia
EUROPEAN PLANE

Other names: English, French plane etc. (according to origin), London plane.

Sources: Europe.

Characteristics of the tree: The tree grows to about 30m (100ft) in height and produces a trunk about 1m (3ft 3in) in diameter. It is widely planted in cities due to its tolerance of pollution, and is easily recognized by its flaking mottled bark.

Characteristics of the wood: A straight-grained wood, with fine to medium texture. It has light reddish-brown heartwood, with distinct darker rays producing attractive fleck figure known as 'lacewood' when quarter-sawn. Similar to but darker than American sycamore (*Platanus occidentalis*). It is a good wood for steam bending. It is perishable and not suitable for exterior use.

Workability: It works well with hand and machine tools. It glues well.

Average dried weight: 640kg/m³ (40lb/ft³).

Finishing: It stains and polishes satisfactorily.

Common uses: Furniture, joinery, turnery, veneer.

Platanus occidentalis
AMERICAN SYCAMORE

Other names: American plane (UK); buttonwood (USA).

Sources: USA.

Characteristics of the tree: A large tree that can grow to 53m (175ft) in height and up to 6m (20ft) in diameter.

Characteristics of the wood: A fine even-textured wood, usually with straight grain. Botanically a plane tree, but lighter in weight than European plane. It is pale brown in colour, with distinct darker rays producing lacewood when quarter-sawn. The wood is perishable and not suitable for exterior use.

Workability: It works well with hand and machine tools, but requires sharp cutters when planing to prevent tearing the ray tissue. It glues well.

Average dried weight: 560kg/m^3 (35lb/ft^3).

Finishing: It stains and polishes satisfactorily.

Common uses: Joinery, furniture, butcher's blocks, doors, panelling, veneer.

Prunus serotina
AMERICAN CHERRY

Other names: Black cherry (Canada, USA); cabinet cherry (USA).

Sources: Canada, USA.

Characteristics of the tree: A tree of moderate size, reaching 21m (70ft) in height, with a trunk about 500mm (1ft 8in) in diameter.

Characteristics of the wood: A hard straight-grained wood, with fine texture. The heartwood is reddish brown to deep red, with brown flecks and some gum pockets. The sapwood is narrow and pink in colour. The wood is moderately strong and durable, and can be steam-bent.

Workability: It works well with hand and machine tools and is a good wood for turning. It glues well.

Average dried weight: 580kg/m³ (36lb/ft³).

Finishing: It takes stain well and can be polished to a fine finish with all types of polish.

Common uses: Furniture, turnery, pattern-making, joinery, musical instruments, tobacco pipes, veneers.

84

Pterocarpus soyauxii
AFRICAN PADAUK

Other names: Camwood, barwood.

Sources: West Africa.

Characteristics of the tree: The tree can grow to a height of 30m (100ft) and produces a buttressed trunk. The diameter above the buttresses can reach 1m (3ft 3in).

Characteristics of the wood: A hard, heavy wood, with straight to interlocked grain and a moderately coarse texture. The heartwood is rich red to purple-brown in colour with red streaks contrasting with the pale-beige sapwood, which can be 200mm (8in) thick. The heartwood is very durable.

Workability: The wood works well and machines to a good finish. It glues well.

Average dried weight: 710kg/m^3 (44lb/ft^3).

Finishing: It polishes to a fine finish.

Common uses: Interior joinery, furniture, turnery, handles, flooring; known as a dyewood.

85

Quercus alba
AMERICAN WHITE OAK

Other names: White oak (USA).

Sources: USA, Canada.

Characteristics of the tree: The tree can reach 30m (100ft) in height and produces a trunk about 1m (3ft 3in) in diameter in good growing conditions.

Characteristics of the wood: Straight-grained with medium-coarse to coarse texture, depending on growing conditions. Similar in appearance to European oak but more variable in colour, it ranges from pale yellow-brown to pale brown and sometimes has a pinkish tint. The wood has good steam-bending properties. It has reasonable durability for outdoor use.

Workability: It works readily with hand and machine tools, and glues satisfactorily.

Average dried weight: 770kg/m³ (48lb/ft³).

Finishing: It stains and polishes well.

Common uses: Building construction, flooring, furniture, interior joinery, plywood, veneer.

Quercus mongolica
JAPANESE OAK

Other names: Ohnara.

Sources: Japan.

Characteristics of the tree: The tree reaches about 30m (100ft) in height, with a straight trunk about 1m (3ft 3in) in diameter.

Characteristics of the wood: A straight-grained and coarse-textured wood, but milder than European and American oak due to its slow, even growth. It is usually light yellowish-brown in colour, has a uniform character, and is generally knot free. The wood has good steam-bending properties. The heartwood is moderately durable for outdoor use.

Workability: It works well with hand and machine tools. Being milder, it is generally easier to work than other white oaks. It glues well.

Average dried weight: 670kg/m^3 (41lb/ft^3).

Finishing: It stains and polishes very well.

Common uses: Furniture, panelling, flooring, boatbuilding, joinery, veneer.

87

Quercus robur
Quercus petraea
EUROPEAN OAK

Other names: English, French, Polish oak etc. (according to country of origin).

Sources: Europe, Asia Minor, North Africa.

Characteristics of the tree: The tree can reach a height of 30m (100ft) or more, depending on growth conditions. It produces a trunk up to 2m (6ft 6in) in diameter.

Characteristics of the wood: A coarse-textured and straight-grained wood, with distinct growth rings and broad rays that give an attractive figure when quarter-sawn. The sapwood is much paler than the pale yellowish-brown colour of the heartwood. It is a tough wood, but oaks grown in Central Europe are lighter and milder than those from Western Europe. The wood is durable but acidic and will cause ferrous metals to corrode. It has good steam-bending properties.

Workability: It works readily with hand and machine tools, but sharp cutting edges need to be maintained. It glues satisfactorily.

Average dried weight: 720kg/m^3 (45lb/ft^3).

Finishing: It can be treated with stain, liming or fuming and finishes well with all types of polish.

Common uses: Furniture, joinery, external woodwork, flooring, carving, boatbuilding, veneer.

Quercus rubra
AMERICAN RED OAK

Other names: Northern red oak.

Sources: Canada, USA.

Characteristics of the tree: The tree reaches a height of up to 21m (70ft) and produces a trunk around 1m (3ft 3in) in diameter depending on growing conditions.

Characteristics of the wood: Straight-grained, with a coarse texture and a less attractive figure than white oak. Although similar to white oak in colour, it generally has a more pinkish-red hue. The texture of red oak can vary according to the rate of growth. Northern-grown wood is milder and not as coarse as the faster-growing red oak of the southern states. The wood has good steam-bending properties. It is not naturally durable.

Workability: It works readily with hand and machine tools, and glues satisfactorily.

Average dried weight: 790kg/m³ (49lb/ft³).

Finishing: It stains and polishes well.

Common uses: Furniture, interior joinery, flooring, decorative veneer, plywood.

Shorea negrosensis
RED LAUAN

Other names: None.

Sources: Philippines.

Characteristics of the tree: A large tree, reaching 50m (165ft) in height and producing a long straight buttressed trunk about 2m (6ft 6in) in diameter.

Characteristics of the wood: A relatively coarse-textured wood, with interlocked grain. The light creamy-coloured sapwood is in contrast with the medium to dark red colour of the heartwood. Quarter-sawn boards display attractive ribbon-grain figure.

Workability: It works easily with hand and machine tools, but the surface can tear when planing. It glues well.

Average dried weight: 630kg/m³ (39lb/ft³).

Finishing: It stains well and can be varnished and polished to a good finish.

Common uses: Interior joinery, boatbuilding, furniture, veneer, scientific instrument boxes.

Swietenia macrophylla
BRAZILIAN MAHOGANY

Other names: Central American, Honduran, Costa Rican, Peruvian mahogany etc. (according to country of origin).

Sources: Central and South America.

Characteristics of the tree: A large tree that can reach 45m (150ft) in height, it produces a long clear but heavily buttressed trunk about 2m (6ft 6in) in diameter.

Characteristics of the wood: A medium-textured wood with straight and even or interlocked grain. The heartwood is reddish brown to deep red. It has good strength-to-weight properties and is naturally durable.

Workability: It works well and cuts cleanly with sharp hand and machine tools. It glues well.

Average dried weight: 560kg/m³ (35lb/ft³).

Finishing: It stains very well and polishes to a fine finish after grain filling.

Common uses: Furniture, interior panelling, joinery, boat planking, carving, pianos, decorative veneer.

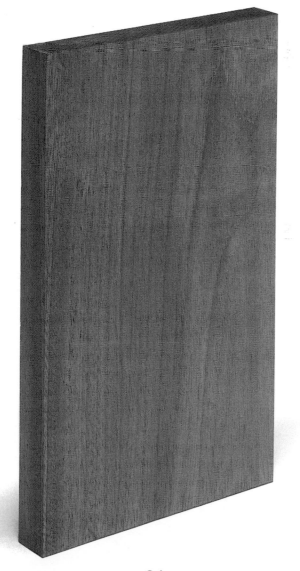

Tectona grandis
TEAK

Other names: Kyun, sagwan, teku, teka.

Sources: South and Southeast Asia, Africa, Caribbean.

Characteristics of the tree: The tree varies in size according to growing conditions, but it can reach 45m (150ft) in height and produce a long straight trunk about 1.5m (5ft) in diameter. The trunk can be fluted and buttressed for support.

Characteristics of the wood: It has a coarse uneven texture with an oily feel. The grain can be straight or wavy, according to its origin. Burma teak is a uniform golden brown; others are darker and more marked. The wood is strong, with moderate steam-bending properties. It is naturally very durable.

Workability: It works well with hand and machine tools, but quickly dulls cutting edges. It glues well on newly prepared surfaces.

Average dried weight: 660kg/m³ (41lb/ft³).

Finishing: It can be stained, varnished and polished, and finishes well with an oil finish.

Common uses: Interior and exterior joinery, boatbuilding, garden furniture, turnery, plywood, veneer.

Tilia americana
BASSWOOD

Other names: American lime.

Sources: Canada, USA.

Characteristics of the tree: A medium-size tree about 20m (65ft) in height and 600mm (2ft) in diameter, but can be more. It produces a straight trunk, often branch-free for much of its length.

Characteristics of the wood: An odourless fine straight-grained even-textured wood, with little contrast between earlywood and latewood. It is creamy white in colour, turning to pale brown on exposure. It is a soft and weak wood, and is lighter in weight than the related European lime (*Tilia vulgaris*). It is not durable.

Workability: An easy wood to work, its fine even texture pares easily with sharp handtools and cuts cleanly with machine tools. It can be brought to a fine smooth finish and it glues well.

Average dried weight: 416kg/m^3 (26lb/ft^3).

Finishing: It stains well and polishes to a fine finish.

Common uses: Carving, turnery, pattern-making, drawing boards, piano keys, plywood, joinery.

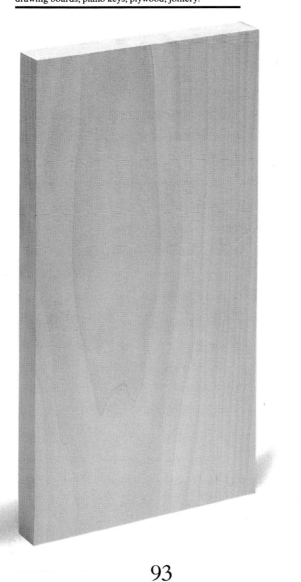

Tilia vulgaris
LIME

Other names: Linden (Germany).

Sources: Europe.

Characteristics of the tree: A tree of moderate size, it reaches about 30m (100ft) in height, but can be more, and produces a clear trunk some 1.2m (4ft) in diameter.

Characteristics of the wood: A soft straight-grained wood, with fine uniform texture. The colour is white to pale yellow, with no distinction between sapwood and heartwood, but darkens to light brown on exposure. It is a strong wood, with good resistance to splitting, and is widely used for fine carving.

Workability: It works very easily with handtools and machines, but requires sharp tools for a clean cut. It is good for turning and excellent for carving. It glues well.

Average dried weight: 560kg/m³ (35lb/ft³).

Finishing: It stains well and polishes to a fine finish.

Common uses: Carving, broom handles, hat blocks, piano sounding boards and keys, harps, turnery, toys.

Triplochiton scleroxylon
OBECHE

Other names: Obechi, arere (Nigeria); wawa (Ghana); samba, wawa (Ivory Coast); ayous (Cameroons).

Sources: West Africa.

Characteristics of the tree: A large heavily buttressed tree, reaching more than 45m (150ft) in height and producing a trunk some 1.5m (5ft) in diameter.

Characteristics of the wood: A lightweight relatively strong wood with fine even texture, though the grain can be interlocked. A rather featureless wood, it is creamy white to pale yellow in colour with little distinction between the sapwood and heartwood. It is not a naturally durable wood.

Workability: An easy wood to work with hand and machine tools, but requires sharp cutting edges as it is rather soft. It glues well.

Average dried weight: 390kg/m^3 (24lb/ft^3).

Finishing: It takes stain and polish well.

Common uses: Interior joinery, drawer linings, furniture, plywood, model-making.

Ulmus americana
AMERICAN WHITE ELM

Other names: Water elm, swamp elm, soft elm (USA); orhamwood (Canada).

Sources: Canada, USA.

Characteristics of the tree: A medium to large tree, depending on growing conditions. Usually it reaches 27m (90ft) in height and 500mm (1ft 8in) in diameter, but can be larger.

Characteristics of the wood: A coarse-textured, strong, tough, medium-density wood. It is usually straight-grained, but can be interlocked. The heartwood is a pale reddish brown. It is a good wood for steam-bending and is generally stronger than European elm.

Workability: The wood can be readily worked with hand and machine tools, but requires sharp cutting edges to give a clean finish. It glues satisfactorily.

Average dried weight: 580kg/m³ (36lb/ft³).

Finishing: It stains and polishes satisfactorily.

Common uses: Boatbuilding, cooperage, furniture, agricultural implements, veneer.

96

Ulmus hollandica
Ulmus procera
DUTCH & ENGLISH ELM

Other names: *Dutch:* Cork bark elm. *English:* Red elm.

Sources: Europe.

Characteristics of the tree: A relatively large tree, reaching 45m (150ft) in height and as much as 2.5m (8ft) in diameter. However, elms are usually cut when they reach around 1m (3ft 3in) in diameter.

Characteristics of the wood: A coarse-textured wood, with distinct irregular growth rings giving attractive figure when plain-sawn. The heartwood is beige-brown in colour. Dutch elm is tougher than English elm, and favourable Continental growing conditions produce wood of more even growth and straighter grain. It is also better for steam bending. Elm wood is not naturally durable. It is sometimes in short supply because of Dutch elm disease.

Workability: Can be fairly difficult to work with hand and machine tools, particularly when planing, if the wood has irregular grain, but it can be brought to a smooth finish. It glues well.

Average dried weight: 560kg/m^3 (35lb/ft^3).

Finishing: The wood stains and polishes well, and is particularly suited to a wax finish.

Common uses: Cabinet furniture, Windsor-chair seats, bentwood backs, turnery, boatbuilding, veneer.

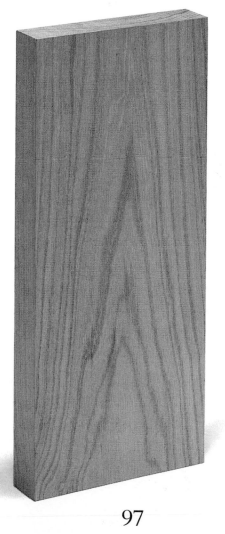

97

Instant guide to common uses
The chart below provides an instant reference to the main uses of all the woods included in this book.

SOFTWOODS

Species	Building construction	Joinery – exterior	Joinery – interior	Doors	Flooring	Furniture/cabinet-making	Turnery	Carving/pattern-making	Musical instruments	Sports equipment	Boxes/crates	Boatbuilding	Tool handles/implements	Common name
Abies alba	○		●		●						●			Silver Fir
Agathis spp.			●		●									Queensland Kauri
Araucaria angustifolia	○		●			●	●							Parana Pine
Araucaria cunninghamii	○		●	●	●	●	●	●			●			Hoop Pine
Cedrus libani	○	●	●	●	●									Cedar of Lebanon
Chamaecyparis nootkatensis	○	●	●	●	●							●	●	Yellow Cedar
Dacrydium cupressinum	○	●	●	●	●									Rimu
Larix decidua	△	●	●	●	●							●	●	Larch
Picea abies	○	●	●		●	●			●		●			Norway Spruce
Picea sitchensis	○		●			●	●		●	●	●	●		Sitka Spruce
Pinus lambertiana	○		●	●							●	●		Sugar Pine
Pinus monticola	○	●	●	●	●		●					●		Western White Pine
Pinus ponderosa	○		●	●	●		●				●	●		Ponderosa Pine
Pinus strobus	○	●	●	●	●				●	●				Yellow Pine
Pinus sylvestris	△	●	●	●	●	●		●			●	●	●	European Redwood
Pseudotsuga menziesii	△	●	●	●	●						●	●		Douglas Fir
Sequoia sempervirens	○	●	●						●		●	●		Sequoia
Taxus baccata			●			●	●	●		●				Yew
Thuja plicata	○	●	●	●							●	●		Western Red Cedar
Tsuga heterophylla	△	●	●	●	●									Western Hemlock

HARDWOODS

Species	Building construction	Joinery – exterior	Joinery – interior	Doors	Flooring	Furniture/cabinet-making	Turnery	Carving/pattern-making	Musical instruments	Sports equipment	Boxes/crates	Boatbuilding	Tool handles/implements	Common name
Acacia melanoxylon			●			●	●		●				●	Australian Blackwood
Acer pseudoplatanus			●	●	●	●	●	●	●	●			●	European Sycamore
Acer rubrum			●	●	●	●	●		●	●				Soft Maple
Acer saccharum			●	●	●	●	●		●	●			●	Hard Maple
Alnus rubra						●	●	●						Red Alder
Astronium fraxinifolium		●				●	●							Gonçalo Alves
Betula alleghaniensis			●	●	●	●	●		●					Yellow Birch
Betula papyrifera						●	●			●	●		●	Paper Birch
Buxus sempervirens						●	●	●	●	●			●	Boxwood
Cardwellia sublimis	□		●		●	●								Silky Oak
Carya illinoensis						●	●			●			●	Pecan Hickory
Castanea dentata		●	●			●					●			American Chestnut
Castanea sativa	○	●	●			●	●							Sweet Chestnut
Castanospermum australe	□		●		●	●	●	●		●			●	Blackbean
Chloroxylon swietenia	□	●	●			●	●							Satinwood
Dalbergia cearensis						●	●							Kingwood
Dalbergia latifolia			●		●	●	●	●	●				●	Indian Rosewood
Dalbergia nigra		●	●	●	●	●	●	●	●				●	Brazilian Rosewood
Dalbergia retusa						●	●						●	Cocobolo
Diospyros ebenum						●	●	●	●	●			●	Ebony
Endiandra palmerstonii		●		●	●	●								Queensland Walnut
Entandrophragma utile	○	●	●	●	●	●			●	●		●		Utile
Eucalyptus marginata	□	●	●	●	●	●						●	●	Jarrah
Fagus grandifolia	○		●	●	●	●	●		●	●		●	●	American Beech
Fagus sylvatica	△		●	●	●	●	●		●	●		●	●	European Beech
Fraxinus americana	○		●	●		●			●	●		●	●	American White Ash
Fraxinus excelsior	○		●	●		●			●	●		●	●	European Ash
Gonystylus macrophyllum			●	●	●	●	●						●	Ramin
Guaiacum officinale						●				●		●	●	Lignum Vitae
Guibourtia demeusei		●	●			●	●						●	Bubinga
Guilandina echinata	□	●	●		●	●	●		●	●				Brazilwood
Juglans cinerea			●		●	●		●			●	●		Butternut
Juglans nigra		●	●	●	●	●	●	●	●	●			●	American Walnut
Juglans regia		●	●	●	●	●	●		●					European Walnut
Liriodendron tulipifera	○	●	●		●		●		●		●			American Whitewood
Ochroma lagopus						●					●			Balsa
Peltogyne spp.	□	●	●		●	●	●			●		●	●	Purpleheart
Pericopsis elata	△	●	●	●	●	●						●	●	Afrormosia
Platanus acerifolia	○		●	●		●	●							European Plane
Platanus occidentalis	○		●	●		●	●							American Sycamore
Prunus serotina			●			●	●	●	●					American Cherry
Pterocarpus soyauxii	□	●	●	●		●	●		●			●	●	African Padauk
Quercus alba	□	●	●	●	●	●	●					●	●	American White Oak
Quercus mongolica	△	●	●	●	●	●	●					●	●	Japanese Oak
Quercus robur/petraea	△	●	●	●	●	●	●					●	●	European Oak
Quercus rubra	△		●	●	●	●						●		American Red Oak
Shorea negrosensis		●	●	●	●			●	●	●	●	●	●	Red Lauan
Swietenia macrophylla	□	●	●	●	●	●	●		●	●	●	●	●	Brazilian Mahogany
Tectona grandis	△	●	●	●	●	●	●					●		Teak
Tilia americana			●			●	●	●	●		●		●	Basswood
Tilia vulgaris			●				●	●	●	●	●		●	Lime
Triplochiton scleroxylon			●			●		●	●	●				Obeche
Ulmus americana	□		●	●		●	●	●				●		American White Elm
Ulmus hollandica/procera	□		●	●		●	●	●				●		Dutch/English Elm

Building construction key: □ = Heavy construction   ○ = Light construction   △ = Light or heavy

VENEERS

Veneers are very thin sheets or 'leaves' of wood which are cut from a log for constructional or decorative purposes. It is ironic that even though veneers of the rarest woods have been used in making some of the finest furniture ever produced, some people still regard veneering as inferior to solid wood. However, few would disagree that veneer, whether selected for its natural colour and figure or worked into floral or formal patterns, brings a unique quality to furniture and woodware. Today, with the widespread use of modern adhesives and stable man-made backing boards, veneered products are superior to solid wood in certain applications. With our natural resources of fine woods gradually disappearing, veneer enables us to use wood economically so we can continue to enjoy it.

VENEER PRODUCTION

The manufacture of veneer requires specialist knowledge. The production starts with the log buyer, who must have the skill to interpret the quality of a log for conversion into commercially viable veneer. Using his judgement and experience, he has to assess the condition of the wood within the log solely on the basis of an external examination.

By looking at the end of the log, the buyer has to determine the quality of the wood, the potential figure of the veneer, the colour, and the ratio of sapwood to heartwood. Other factors that will affect the value of the log must also be noted, including the presence and extent of any staining and any weaknesses or defects such as shakes, ingrown bark or excessive knots and resin ducts or pockets. Much of this information will be revealed by the first cut through the length of the log – but the buyer has, of course, to purchase the log before it is cut.

Once the log has been purchased and delivered to the sawmill, it is the expertise of the veneer cutter that counts, since it is the veneer cutter who has to decide the best way to convert the wood to yield the maximum number of high-quality veneers.

Grading

As decorative veneers are cut, they are taken from the slicer and stacked in sequence. The veneers then pass through a drying process before being graded. Most species are 'clipped' on a guillotine to trim them into regular shapes and sizes. Others, such as yew or burr veneer, are left as they are cut from the log.

Veneers are priced according to their size and quality. They are checked for natural or milling defects, thickness, type of figure and colour, for example, and graded accordingly. A particular log may yield veneers of various value. The better veneers are graded as 'face quality' and have a greater value than the narrower or poorer 'backing grade'.

The veneers are kept in multiples of four for matching purposes and bound into 'bundles' of 16, 24, 28 or 32 leaves. The bundles are restacked in consecutive order and the reassembled log is stored in a cool warehouse ready for sale.

CUTTING VENEER

Veneer logs are cut from the main stem of the tree between the root butt and the first branch. The bark is removed and the log checked for foreign matter such as nails.

Before the log is converted into veneer it is softened by immersion in hot water or by steaming. The whole log may be treated, or it may first be cut by a huge bandsaw into 'flitches' to suit the veneer-cutting method. The duration of this conditioning is controlled according to the type and hardness of the wood and the thickness of the veneer to be cut. It may be a matter of days or weeks. Pale woods such as maple are not pre-treated, as the process would discolour the veneer.

There are basically three methods for cutting veneer: saw cutting, rotary cutting and flat slicing.

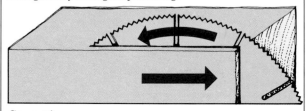

Saw cutting

Until the early eighteenth century, when veneer-slicing machines were developed, all veneers were cut using first handsaws and then power saws. These veneers were relatively thick, some being about 3mm ($\frac{1}{8}$in).

Sawn veneers, although wasteful of material, are still cut by huge circular saws, but only for special or difficult-to-work irregular-grained woods such as curls or where it proves the most economical method. They are usually about 1 to 1.2mm ($\frac{1}{25}$ to $\frac{1}{21}$in) thick.

You can use your workshop bandsaw or table saw to produce strips of veneer for laminating purposes, particularly if this proves to be more economical or will provide you with material better suited to your needs than the veneers that are commercially available.

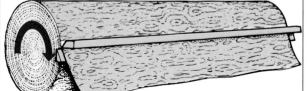

Rotary cutting

Constructional veneers of softwood and some hardwoods are cut by the rotary peeling method. The whole log is set in a huge lathe which peels off a continuous sheet of veneer.

The log is rotated against a pressure bar and knife which run the full length of the machine. The knife is set just below the bar and forward of it by the thickness of the veneer. The setting of the bar and knife in relation to the log is critical, to prevent surface failures known as 'checks'. For each revolution of the log, the knife is automatically advanced by the thickness of the veneer.

Veneer produced in this way can be recognised by a distinctive watery-patterned figure where the continuous tangential cut has sliced through the growth rings.

Rotary cutting is a particularly efficient way to produce veneers suitable for the manufacture of man-made boards, as they can be cut to any width.

Although primarily used for the manufacture of constructional veneers, the method is also used to produce decorative veneers such as bird's-eye maple.

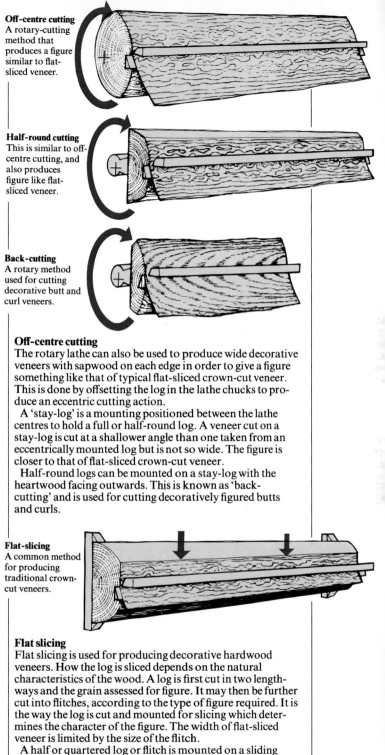

Off-centre cutting
A rotary-cutting method that produces a figure similar to flat-sliced veneer.

Half-round cutting
This is similar to off-centre cutting, and also produces figure like flat-sliced veneer.

Back-cutting
A rotary method used for cutting decorative butt and curl veneers.

Off-centre cutting

The rotary lathe can also be used to produce wide decorative veneers with sapwood on each edge in order to give a figure something like that of typical flat-sliced crown-cut veneer. This is done by offsetting the log in the lathe chucks to produce an eccentric cutting action.

A 'stay-log' is a mounting positioned between the lathe centres to hold a full or half-round log. A veneer cut on a stay-log is cut at a shallower angle than one taken from an eccentrically mounted log but is not so wide. The figure is closer to that of flat-sliced crown-cut veneer.

Half-round logs can be mounted on a stay-log with the heartwood facing outwards. This is known as 'back-cutting' and is used for cutting decoratively figured butts and curls.

Flat-slicing
A common method for producing traditional crown-cut veneers.

Flat slicing

Flat slicing is used for producing decorative hardwood veneers. How the log is sliced depends on the natural characteristics of the wood. A log is first cut in two lengthways and the grain assessed for figure. It may then be further cut into flitches, according to the type of figure required. It is the way the log is cut and mounted for slicing which determines the character of the figure. The width of flat-sliced veneer is limited by the size of the flitch.

A half or quartered log or flitch is mounted on a sliding frame which can move up and down. The pressure bar and knife are set horizontally in front of the wood, and a slice of veneer is removed with every down stroke of the frame. After each cut the knife or flitch is advanced by the required thickness of the veneer.

A flat-sliced half-round log produces the crown-cut veneers commonly used in cabinet work. They have the same attractive figure as tangentially cut flat-sawn boards.

Woods that display striking and attractive figure when radially cut are converted into quarter-cut or near quarter-cut flitches. These are mounted with the rays of the wood following the direction of the cut as closely as possible, to produce the maximum number of radially cut veneers.

Quartered flitches can also be mounted to produce tangentially cut flat-sliced veneer. These are narrower than crown-cut veneers cut from half-round logs but can display attractive figure.

Quarter-cut slicing
Used to produce veneers displaying attractive quarter-cut figure.

Flat-sliced quartered
Quartered logs are sometimes cut tangentially to make flat-sliced veneers.

KNIFE CHECKS

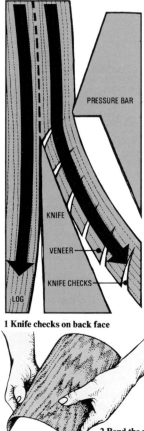

PRESSURE BAR

KNIFE

VENEER

KNIFE CHECKS

LOG

1 Knife checks on back face

2 Bend the veneer as a test

Veneer-slicing machines are like giant planes, with the veneer representing the shaving. In this case it is important that the 'shaving' is produced to a fine tolerance and with a clean cut. The quality of the cut is controlled by the pressure bar and knife setting (1).

Fine cracks known as 'knife checks' can occur on the back face of the veneer, particularly when rotary-peeled. The back face of the veneer is called the 'open' or 'loose' face; and the other, the 'closed' or 'tight' face. You can identify the faces by flexing the veneer, which will bend to a greater degree when the open face is convex (2).

Always try to lay veneer with the open face down, since the slightly coarser surface does not finish quite so well as the closed face. This is not always possible, however, for when laying book-matched veneers it is necessary to turn alternate veneers over.

TYPES OF VENEER

*The veneer-manufacturing process makes available a wide choice of hardwoods, many of which are uneconomic or unsuitable for use in 'solid' form. A tree can be converted into various types of decorative veneer. The figure depends not only on the natural features of the wood, such as colour, grain and texture, but also on which part of the tree is used and how it is cut into veneer. Most **veneer** is cut from the main trunk, which gives the longest and usually the widest-figured veneers. The **variety** of types is obtained by slicing the log in different ways. The type description may refer to the method of cutting – as in 'crown-cut walnut' – or to the part of the tree from which the veneer is cut, as in 'burr' or 'burl' veneer. Most sliced veneer is cut about 0.6mm ($\frac{1}{42}$in) thick. Thicker veneer for furniture restoration is also produced in some woods.*

BUYING VENEER

You can buy single leaves or full bundles of veneer from specialist suppliers and from some timber merchants, either by mail order or directly. Because it is important to keep the veneers in consecutive order for matching purposes, you will be supplied with veneer from the top of the stack. The merchant will not usually pull out selected leaves, as that would reduce the value of the veneer flitch.

Before buying veneer, calculate the area you need and make an allowance for wastage. Err on the generous side – since each veneer is unique and if you have to order more you are unlikely to obtain a match. Full leaves are customarily priced by the square foot, and some merchants will supply pre-cut lengths at a set price per piece. Selected small pieces of veneer are available in specialist packs for marquetry.

Small orders of full veneers supplied through the mail are usually rolled for dispatch. Small pieces of veneer, such as burrs or curls, are generally packed flat – but they can also be sent with a package of rolled veneer, in which case they may be dampened to allow them to bend without breaking. Since veneers are fragile, open a rolled package carefully, so that it doesn't spring open and cause damage. End splits are not uncommon in veneer. Repair them promptly with gummed paper tape (particularly light-coloured woods) to prevent dirt entering.

If the veneer remains curled after unpacking, dampen it with steam from a kettle or pass it through a tray of water, then press it flat between sheets of chipboard. Do not leave it between boards in a damp condition, or mildew may develop. Store veneers flat and protect them from dust and strong light, as wood is light-sensitive and can lighten or darken according to the species.

1 Crotch	3 Burr or burl
2 Trunk	4 Stump or butt

Parts of the tree used for veneers

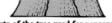

Part of tree: Burr

Method of cutting
Rotary-cut or flat-sliced

Burr or burl veneer
Burrs or burls are abnormal growths on the
trunk of a tree. Burr veneers display an
attractive pattern of tightly packed bud
formations that appear as rings and dots.
They are relatively expensive veneers and are
highly prized for furniture and small woodware. Burr veneers are supplied in irregular
shapes and various sizes, from 150 × 100mm
(6 × 4in) to about 1m (3ft 3in) long by 450mm
(1ft 6in) wide.

Top to bottom
Elm burr
Thuya burr
Ash burr

Butt veneers

Butt veneers are cut from the stump, or butt, of certain trees. Highly figured veneers, caused by the distorted grain, occur by back-cutting on a rotary lathe. Like burr or burl veneers, they are fragile and can contain holes where small pieces have become detached. Where these cannot be avoided, pieces of veneer can be patched in to make a repair. Matching filler can be applied to very small holes after laying.

Part of tree: Stump

Method of cutting
Rotary back-cut

Top to bottom
American walnut butt veneer
Ash butt veneer
American walnut burry-butt veneer

Coloured veneer

Artificially coloured veneers are available from specialist suppliers. Light-coloured woods, such as sycamore, are used. 'Harewood' is chemically treated sycamore which turns silver-grey to dark-grey. Dyes are used to produce other colours, the veneer being pressure-treated for maximum penetration.

Method of colouring
Harewood (sycamore) is immersed in a solution of ferrous sulphate. Commercially colour-dyed woods are processed in an autoclave.

Left to right
Blue-dyed veneer
Turquoise-dyed veneer
Green-dyed veneer
Chemically coloured 'harewood'

Crown-cut veneer

Tangentially cut flat-sliced veneer is known as 'crown-cut'. It displays an attractive figure of bold sweeping curves and ovals along the centre of the leaf, with striped grain nearer the edges. Crown-cut veneer is produced in lengths of 2.4m (8ft) or more and in various widths, ranging from about 225mm (9in) to 600mm (2ft), depending on species. It is used for furniture-making and wall panelling.

Part of tree: Trunk

Method of cutting
Flat-sliced

Left to right
Crown-cut kingwood
Crown-cut Brazilian rosewood
Crown-cut ash
Crown-cut American walnut

Part of tree: Trunk

Method of cutting
Flat-sliced

Curly-figured veneer

Wavy-grained woods produce veneers with subtle bands of light and dark grain running across the width of the leaf. Fiddleback sycamore and ripple ash are two examples. The 'fiddleback' sycamore is so called because the wood is traditionally used for making violin backs. The veneer is used for cabinet doors and panels where a striking decorative effect with a horizontal emphasis is required.

Left to right
'Fiddleback' sycamore
Ripple ash

Curl veneer

Curl veneer is cut from the 'crotch' or 'fork' of a tree where the trunk divides. When the crotch is sliced perpendicularly an attractive figure is revealed. The distorted diverging grain produces a lustrous upward-sweeping plume pattern known as 'feather figure'. It is available in sizes from 300mm to 1m (1ft to 3ft 3in) long and 200 to 450mm (8in to 1ft 6in) wide.

Part of tree: Crotch

Method of cutting
Rotary back-cut

Top to bottom
Mahogany curl
European walnut curl

Part of tree: Trunk

Method of cutting
Rotary –cut
(peeled)

Freak-figured veneer

Hardwood logs with irregular growth may be
rotary-cut to produce veneer displaying
various patterns. Bird's-eye maple and masur
birch are examples. The features of the masur
birch are caused by wood-boring insect larvae
which attack the cambium layer of the tree
producing the distinct brown markings. Irregular-
grained woods can also produce veneer with
'blistered figure' and 'quilted figure'.

Left to right
Quilted makoré
Masur birch
Bird's-eye maple
Quilted willow

110

Ray-figured veneer

Woods with pronounced ray-cell structure, such as oak and plane, have striking figure when quarter-cut. The distinct wide bands of ray cells in oak produce highly prized 'ray-fleck' or 'splash' figure. Quarter-cut plane veneer is known as 'lacewood' and displays speckled or fine wavy-grain figure. Quarter-cut veneer is produced in lengths up to 2.4m (8ft) and in various widths ranging from 150mm (6in) to 350mm (1ft 2in) depending on species. It is used for furniture-making and panelling.

Part of tree: Trunk

Method of cutting
Quarter-cut flat-sliced

Left to right
Quarter-cut silky oak
Quarter-cut 'lacewood'
Quarter-cut 'ray-fleck' oak

111

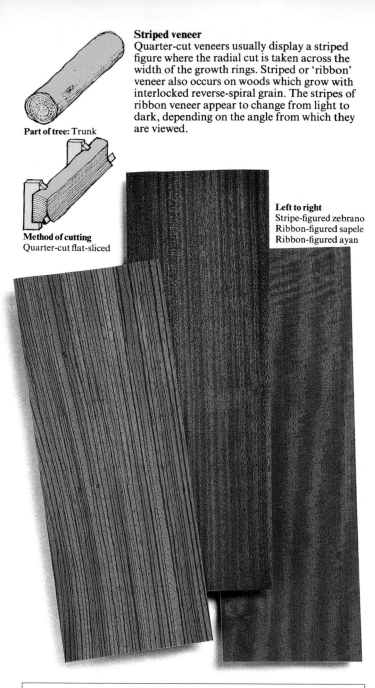

Striped veneer

Quarter-cut veneers usually display a striped figure where the radial cut is taken across the width of the growth rings. Striped or 'ribbon' veneer also occurs on woods which grow with interlocked reverse-spiral grain. The stripes of ribbon veneer appear to change from light to dark, depending on the angle from which they are viewed.

Part of tree: Trunk

Method of cutting
Quarter-cut flat-sliced

Left to right
Stripe-figured zebrano
Ribbon-figured sapele
Ribbon-figured ayan

Micro-thin veneer

Microwood is an ultra-thin natural-wood veneer, 0.1mm (0.004in) thick, bonded to a self-adhesive paper backing. It is available in a range of hardwoods in natural and pre-stained finishes and produced in sheets and rolls. It is easily cut with scissors or a craft knife for marquetry work, and can be formed around small radii and slight compound curves without splitting. It bonds readily to a wide range of backing materials.

BANDINGS

Bandings and inlays can transform a plain panel into an attractive piece of decorative woodwork in the traditional manner. Bandings are plain or patterned strips of veneer used to create decorative borders. You can make your own, but commercially produced bandings offer a wide choice and come ready to use.

LINES AND BANDINGS

Commercially produced decorative inlay bandings are made in batches from selected woods. Always buy sufficient when you first order, as you may not be able to obtain an exact match at a later date. Not only will the wood be different but the size may vary, too.

Stringing lines
Stringings are fine strips of wood used to divide areas of veneer by providing light or dark lines between different types of veneer or where the grain direction changes. Ebony and boxwood were the traditional materials for stringings, but nowadays black-dyed wood is used instead of ebony.

Bandings
Decorative bandings are made from side-grain sections of coloured woods glued together and sliced to produce strips approximately 1mm ($\frac{1}{25}$ in) thick. They come ready-edged, with a choice of boxwood or black stringings, and are used to make ornamental borders.

Strips of veneer cut across the grain are known as cross-bandings and are used to make bordered panels. Make cross-bandings yourself, cutting them from the veneer used for the panel.

Stringing lines

Decorative bandings

113

INLAY MOTIFS

Inlays are marquetry motifs used as decorative features; they are available in traditional, pictorial or floral patterns. Commercially made inlays are relatively simple to apply either to veneered or solid-wood surfaces. You can hand-lay individual motifs, but use cauls for veneer assemblies.

Inlay motifs are supplied with a protective paper backing. They are laid with the paper surface uppermost. Some are made to a finished size and shape, others have spare veneer surrounding the design for cutting to shape.

Surface laying
Motifs can be glued directly onto a solid-wood surface without inlaying them. To improve the appearance, gouge a groove around the edge to give a shadow break line.

MAN-MADE BOARDS

Man-made boards are relatively new and have been taken up enthusiastically by industry and the home woodworker alike. Board manufacturers are constantly developing their products with a view to improving quality, economy of raw materials and ease of working. Consequently, there is a wide range of boards available today. These fall into roughly three categories: laminated boards, particle boards and fibreboards. As new products are introduced, some kinds of laminated boards, such as solid-core blockboard, may be replaced by cheaper particle-board and fibreboard types.

PLYWOOD BOARDS

Plywood is a laminated material made from thin sheets of wood known as construction veneers, plies or laminates, which are bonded in layers to form a strong stable board. Laminating wood was a technique known to craftsmen in ancient times, but plywood is a relatively modern material first produced commercially around the mid-nineteenth century. Its panel size, stability and ease of working made it a useful material for interior joinery and carcass construction, but it was not until the development of waterproof adhesives in the 1930s that it found a place in the construction industry.

Plywood construction

A board of solid wood is relatively unstable and will shrink or swell to a greater degree across the fibres than it will along them. In so doing it is also likely to distort, depending on how it is cut from the tree. The tensile strength of wood is greatest following the direction of the fibres, but it will also readily split with the grain.

Plywood is constructed with the fibres or grain of alternate plies set at right angles to one another to counter movement of the wood. This produces a stable warp-resisting board which has no natural direction of cleavage. The greatest strength of a panel is usually parallel to the face grain.

Most plywood is made with an odd number of plies to give a balanced construction, three being the minimum. The number varies according to the thickness of the plies and the finished board. Whatever the number, the construction must be symmetrical about the centre ply or the centre line of the panel thickness.

The surface veneers of a typical plywood board are known as 'face plies'. Where the quality of one of the outer plies is better than the other, the better ply is called 'the face' and the other 'the back'. The grade of the face plies is usually specified by a letter code. The perpendicularly laid plies immediately beneath the face plies are known as 'cross-bandings'. The centre ply (or plies) is known as 'the core'.

Sizes

Plywood is made in a wide range of sizes. The thickness of commercially available plywood generally ranges from 3mm ($\frac{1}{8}$in) to 30mm ($1\frac{3}{16}$in), in approximately 3mm ($\frac{1}{8}$in) increments. Thinner 'aircraft plywood' is available from specialist suppliers.

The typical width of a board is 1.22m (4ft), but 1.52m (5ft) boards are also available. The most common length is 2.44m (8ft), although boards up to 3.66m (12ft) are made. The dimensions are expressed in imperial or metric measurements depending on the source of manufacture or supply.

The grain of the face ply usually follows the longest dimension of the board, but not always. Normally, it runs parallel to the first dimension quoted by the manufacturer. Thus a 1.22 × 2.44m (4 × 8ft) board will have the grain running across the width.

BONDING

The performance of plywood is determined not only by the quality of the plies but also by the type of adhesive used in its manufacture. Plywoods can be grouped according to usage.

Interior plywood (INT)
Plywoods of this grade should be used only for non-structural interior applications. They are generally produced with an appearance-grade face ply and a poorer quality for the back.

INT plywoods are manufactured with urea-formaldehyde adhesive, which is light in colour. Most boards are suitable for use in dry conditions, such as furniture or wall panelling. Modified adhesive employed in the manufacture of certain types of board affords them some degree of moisture resistance, enabling them to be used in areas of high humidity. Never use interior-grade plywood for exterior applications.

Exterior plywood
Exterior-grade plywoods can be used for fully or semi-exposed conditions (depending on the quality of the adhesive), where structural performance is not required.

Boards suitable for fully exposed conditions are bonded with dark-coloured phenol-formaldehyde (phenolic) adhesive. This type produces 'weather and boil proof' (WBP) plywood. WBP adhesives comply with an established standard and systematic tests, as well as their record in service over many years, have proved them to be highly resistant to weather, micro-organisms, cold and boiling water, steam and dry heat.

Exterior-grade plywoods are also produced using melamine urea-formaldehyde adhesive. This type of board is semi-durable under exposed conditions.

Exterior-grade plywood is a good material for kitchen fitments and for applications around showers or bathrooms.

Marine plywood
Marine plywood is a high-quality face-graded structural plywood primarily produced for marine use. It is constructed from selected plies from a limited range of mahogany-type woods. Marine ply has no 'voids', or gaps, and is bonded with a durable phenolic (WBP) adhesive. It can also be used for interior fitments.

Structural plywood
Structural or engineering-grade plywood is manufactured for applications where strength and durability are the prime consideration. It is bonded with phenolic resin adhesive. An appearance-grade face ply of a lower quality is used, and the boards may not be sanded.

TYPES OF PLYWOOD

Different types of plywood are produced for such diverse applications as agricultural installations, aircraft and marine construction, structural building work, interior fitments, toys and furniture. Performance and suitability of application depend on species of wood, type of bond and grade of veneer.

Plywood boards are manufactured in many parts of the world and the species of wood used varies according to place of origin. The face veneers and core may be made from different species or the boards may be constructed from the same species throughout.

Softwood boards are commonly made from Douglas fir or various species of pine, common hardwood types from light-coloured temperate woods such as birch, beech and basswood. Tropical woods used for plywood construction include lauan, meranti and gaboon, all of which are red in colour.

APPEARANCE GRADING

Plywood producers employ a coding system to grade the quality of the plies used in the manufacture of their boards.

A typical system uses the letters A, B, C, C-plugged and D. The A grade is the best quality, being smooth-cut with virtually no defects. The D grade is the poorest, having the maximim amount of permitted defects such as knots, holes, splits and discoloration.

The letters quoted or stamped on the board refer to the appearance of the face plies only and do not indicate the structural performance of the board. An A-A grade plywood has two good faces, while a B-C board has poorer-grade outer plies (the better B grade being the face and the C grade the back). Decorative plywoods are faced with selected matched veneers, and are referred to by the wood species used for the face veneer.

Typical grading stamps

Panels with A-grade or B-grade veneer on one side only are usually stamped on the back of the panel. Those with both sides faced with A or B veneers usually carry the mark on the edge of the panel.

1 **Trademark of the grading authority**
American Plywood Association.

2 **Panel grade**
Identifies the grade of the veneer on the face and back of the panel.

3 **Mill number**
Code number of producing mill.

4 **Species group number**
Group 1 represents the strongest species.

5 **Exposure classification**
Indicates bond durability.

6 **Product Standard number**
Indicates the panel meets the U.S. Product Standard.

Stamp applied to back face.

Stamp applied to edge.

Decorative plywood
is faced with selected
flat-sliced or quarter-
cut matched veneers,
usually of hardwoods
such as afrormosia,
beech, cherry or oak,
and is mainly used for
panelling. A balancing
veneer of lesser quality
is applied to the back
of the board.

Three-ply board
has the face veneers
bonded to a single core
veneer. Their thickness
may be the same, or the
core may be thicker to
improve the balance of
the construction. This
type is sometimes called
'balanced' or 'solid
core' plywood. Thin
three-ply boards are
used for drawer bottoms
and cabinet backs.

Drawerside plywood
is the exception to the
cross-banding con-
struction method. This
type has the grain of all
the plies running in the
same direction. It is
made of hardwood to a
nominal thickness of
12mm ($\frac{1}{2}$in) and is used
for drawer sides in place
of solid wood.

Decorative

Drawerside

Three-ply 118

Multi-ply

has a core consisting of an odd number of plies. The thickness of each ply may be the same, or the cross-banded ones may be thicker. This helps give the board equal stiffness in its length and width. It is a good material for use in making veneered furniture.

Multi-ply

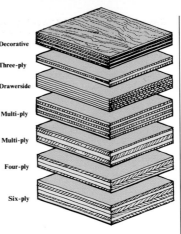

Decorative

Three-ply

Drawerside

Multi-ply

Multi-ply

Four-ply

Six-ply

● **Four-ply and six-ply**
Four-ply has two thick-cut plies bonded together, with their grain in the same direction and perpendicular to the face plies. This type is stiffer in one direction and is usually used for structural work. Six-ply (shown here) is similar to four-ply in construction but has the core parallel to the face, with cross-banded ply in between.

STORING AND FIXING BOARDS

Storing boards
To save space, store boards on edge. Make a rack to keep the edges clear of the floor and support the boards evenly at a slight angle. When storing thin boards, support the full area of each board with a thicker board underneath.

Fixing boards
Screw-fixings in the edges of man-made boards are not as strong or secure as those made in the face.

Drill pilot holes in the edge of plywood to prevent splitting. The diameter of the screws used should not exceed 25 per cent of the board's thickness.

Blockboard and lamin-board will hold screws well in the side edges, but not in the end grain.

Screw-holding in chip-board depends on the density of the board. It is usually relatively weak, but special chipboard screws hold better than standard wood screws. Always drill pilot holes, both for face-fixing and edge-fixing. Use special fastenings or inserts for improved holdings.

BLOCKBOARD AND LAMINBOARD

Blockboard is a form of plywood, being of laminated construction. It differs from conventional plywood in that the core is constructed from strips of solid wood cut approximately square in section and edge-butted, but not glued. The core is faced with one or two layers of ply on each side.

Laminboard is similar to blockboard but the core is constructed from narrow strips approximately 5mm ($\frac{3}{16}$in) wide, which are usually edge-glued.

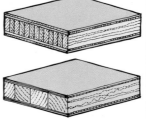

Laminboard *(Left)*
is superior to blockboard for veneer work, as the core is less likely to show through. It is also more expensive. Boards of three-ply and five-ply construction are produced. The plies of the five-ply type may either be perpendicular to the core or cross-banded.
Blockboard *(Right)*
is a stiff material suitable for furniture applications, particularly shelving and worktops. It makes a good substrate for veneer work, but the core strips can 'telegraph' (i.e. show through).

PARTICLE BOARDS

Wood-particle boards are made from small chips or flakes of wood bonded together under pressure. Various types are produced according to the shape and size of the particles, their distribution through the thickness of the board and the type of adhesive used to bind them together. Softwoods are generally used, although a proportion of hardwood material is sometimes included.

Types of board
Particle boards are stable and uniformly consistent materials. Those constructed with fine particles have featureless surfaces and are highly suitable as groundwork for veneer. A wide range of pre-veneered decorative boards using wood, paper foil or plastic laminates are available. Most particle boards are relatively brittle and have a lower tensile strength than plywood.

Chipboard
Most types of particle board of interest to the woodworker are of interior quality, commonly known as chipboard. Chipboard, like other wood products, is adversely affected by excess moisture – the board swells in its thickness and on drying does not recover. However, moisture-resistant types suitable for flooring or wet conditions are made.

Single-layer chipboard
(Left)
is made from a mat of similar-sized particles evenly distributed throughout. It has a relatively coarse surface. This type is suitable for wood veneer or plastic laminate, although not for painting.

Three-layer chipboard
(Right)
has a core layer of coarse particles sandwiched between two outside layers of fine high-density particles. The outer layers contain a higher proportion of resin, which produces a smooth surface suitable for most finishes.

121

1 Graded-density chipboard has surfaces of very fine particles and a core of coarser particles. Unlike layered types, there is a gradual transition from the coarse particles to the fine surface.

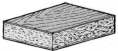

2 Decorative chipboard is manufactured with a facing of selected wood veneer, plastic laminate or a thin melamine foil. The wood-veneered boards are sanded ready for polishing, the foil-faced and plastic-laminated boards need no finishing. Some plastic-laminated boards for worktops are made with finished profiled edges, while matching edging strips are available for lipping melamine-faced and wood-veneered boards.

TYPES OF LIPPING

The edges of man-made boards must be finished with a lipping to cover the core material. You can use either long-grain or cross-grain veneer or a more substantial solid-wood lipping of matching or contrasting timber. Lippings can be applied before or after surface veneering. In the case of pre-veneered boards you have no choice but to lip the edge last.

Applying lippings

The simplest edging to apply is the pre-glued veneer type which is ironed onto the edge. These edge lippings are primarily sold for finishing veneered chipboard panels and are available in a limited range of matching veneer.

For a more substantial edging, and one which can be shaped, cut thick lippings from matching solid wood. Butt-joint the lipping to the edge or tongue and groove it for greater strength.

Mitre the corners of thick lippings to improve the finished appearance. This is particularly necessary if the edge is moulded.

When gluing up a long lipping, use a stiff batten between the lipping and the cramp heads to help spread the clamping forces over the full length of the work.

When planing glued-on edge lippings to width, take care not to touch the surface veneer, particularly when working across the direction of the grain.

1

122

3 Oriented-strand board is a three layered material made from long strands of pine. The strands in each layer are laid in one direction, and each layer is perpendicular to the next in the same manner as plywood.

4 Flakeboard or waferboard uses large shavings of wood which are laid horizontally and overlap one another. These boards have greater tensile strength than standard chipboard.

2

3

4

FIBREBOARDS

Fibreboards are made from wood that has been reduced to its basic fibre elements and reconstituted to make a stable homogeneous material. Boards of various density are produced, according to the pressure applied and the adhesive used in their manufacture.

Medium boards

Medium boards are made in a similar way to hardboard. They are produced in two grades. Low-density (LM) board, 6 to 12mm ($\frac{1}{4}$ to $\frac{1}{2}$ in) thick, is used for pinboard or wall panelling. High-density (HM) board is stronger and is used for interior panelling.

Medium–density fibreboard (MDF) is a fibreboard with two

smooth faces manufactured by a dry process. The fibres are bonded together with a synthetic-resin adhesive. It has a uniform structure and a fine texture which allows the edges and faces to be cleanly profile-machined.

This type of fibreboard can be worked like wood and can be used as a substitute for solid wood in some applications. It makes an excellent substrate for veneer and takes paint finishes well.

MDF boards are made in thicknesses of 6 to 32mm ($\frac{1}{4}$ to $1\frac{1}{4}$in) and a wide range of panel sizes.

Medium boards
(From left to right)
High-density
(HM) board
Low-density
(LM) board
Medium-density
fibreboard (MDF)
Oak-veneered
MDF board

Hardboards
(From left to right)
Standard hardboard
Tempered hardboard
Embossed hardboard
Decorative-faced hardboard
Perforated hardboard

124

Hardboards

Hardboard is a high-density fibreboard produced from wet fibres pressed at high pressure and temperature. The natural resins in the fibres are used to bond them together.

Tempered hardboard is a standard-density board which has been impregnated with resin and oil to produce a stronger material that is water-and-abrasion-resistant.
Standard hardboard has only one smooth face. It is made in a wide range of thicknesses from 1.5 to 12mm ($\frac{1}{16}$ to $\frac{1}{2}$in),
A cheap material, it is commonly used for drawer bottoms and cabinet backs.
Duo-faced hardboard is similar to standard hardboard but has two smooth faces.
Decorative hardboard is produced in the form of perforated, moulded or lacquered boards.

125

Air drying
A method for seasoning timber that permits covered stacks of sawn wood to dry naturally in the open air.

Autoclave
A sealed pressure vessel used in the production of dyed veneer.

Backing grade
The category of cheaper veneers that are glued to the back of a board in order to balance better-quality veneers glued to the front face.

Banding
A plain or patterned strip of veneer used to make decorative borders.

Blockboard
a man-made building board with a core of approximately square-section solid-wood strips sandwiched between thin plywood sheets. *See also* laminboard.

Burl
See burr.

Burr
A warty growth on the trunk of a tree. When sliced it produces speckled burr veneer. *or* An extremely thin strip of metal left along the cutting edge of a blade after honing or grinding.

Buttressed
Having roughly triangular outgrowths at the base of the trunk to give increased stability.

Case-hardened
A term used to describe unevenly seasoned timber with a moisture content that varies throughout its thickness.

Cauls
Sheets of wood or metal used to press veneer onto groundwork.

Checks
Splits in timber caused by uneven seasoning. *See also* knife checks.

Chipboard
A mat of small particles of wood and glue compressed into a flat building board.

Clear timber
Good-quality wood that is free from defects.

Close grain
A term used to describe wood with small pores or fine cell structure. Also known as fine textured.

Coarse-textured
See open grain.

Comb-grain
Another term for quarter-sawn.

Core
The central layer of plies, particles or wooden strips in a man-made board.

Cross-banding
Strips of veneer cut across the grain and used as decorative borders.

Cross grain
Grain that deviates from the main axis of a workpiece or tree.

Crotch figure
Another term for curl figure.

Crown-cut
A term used to describe veneer that has been tangentially sliced from a log, producing oval or curved grain patterns.

Cup
To bend as a result of shrinkage – specifically across the width of a piece of wood.

Curl figure
The grain pattern on wood that has been cut from that part of a tree where a branch joins the main stem or trunk.

Curly figure
See curly grain.

Curly grain
Wood grain exhibiting an irregular wavy pattern.

Dimension stock
Prepared timber cut to standard sizes.

Dressed stock
Another term for dimension stock.

Earlywood
That part of a tree's annual growth rings that is laid down in the early part of the growing season.

Edge-grain
Another term for quarter-sawn.

End grain
The surface of wood exposed after cutting across the fibres.

Face quality
A term used to describe better-quality veneers that are used to cover the visible surfaces of a workpiece.

Fibreboards
A range of building boards made from reconstituted wood fibres.

Figure
Another term for grain pattern.

Fine textured
See close grain.

Flat-grain
Another term for plain-sawn.

Flat sliced
A term used to describe a sheet of knife-cut veneer produced on a machine with a sliding action.

Flat-sawn
Another term for plain-sawn.

Flitches
Pieces of wood sawn from a log for slicing into veneers. *or* The bundle of sliced veneers.

Grain
The general direction or arrangement of the fibrous materials of wood.

Green wood
Newly cut timber that has not been seasoned.

Groundwork
The backing material to which veneer is glued.

Hardwood
Wood cut from broadleaved, mostly deciduous, trees which belong to the botanical group Angiospermae.

Heartwood
The mature wood that forms the spine of a tree.

Inlay
To insert pieces of wood or metal into prepared recesses so that the material lies flush with the surrounding surfaces. *or* The piece of material itself.

Interlocked grain
Bands of annual rings with alternating left-hand and right-hand spiral grain.

In wind
See winding.

Kiln drying
A method for seasoning timber using a mixture of hot air and steam.

Knife checks
Splits across veneer caused by poorly adjusted veneer-slicing equipment.

Laminate
A component made from thin strips of wood glued together. *or* To glue strips together to form a component.

Laminboard
A man-made building board with a core of narrow strips of wood glued together and sandwiched between thin plywood sheets. *See also* blockboard.

Latewood
That part of a tree's annual growth ring that is laid down in the latter part of the growing season.

Lipping
A protective strip of solid wood applied to the edge of a man-made-board panel or table top.

Long grain
Grain that is aligned with the main axis of a workpiece. *See also* short grain.

Marquetry
The process of laying relatively small pieces of veneer to make decorative patterns or pictures. *See also* parquetry.

Mild
Easy to work.

Open grain
A term used to describe ring-porous wood with large pores. Also known as coarse-textured.

Parquetry
A similar process to marquetry but using veneers cut into geometric shapes to make decorative patterns.

Particle boards
Building boards made from small chips of wood bonded together with glue under pressure.

PEG
Polyethylene glycol – a stabilizing agent used in place of conventional seasoning processes to treat green timber.

Photosynthesis
A natural process that takes place when energy in the form of light is absorbed by chlorophyll, producing the nutrients on which plants live.

Plain-sawn
A term used to describe a piece of wood with growth rings that meet the faces of the board at angles of less than 45 degrees. *See also* rift-sawn.

Plywood
A building board made by bonding a number of wood veneers together under pressure.

Quarter-sawn
A term used to describe a piece of wood with growth rings at not less than 45 degrees to the faces of the board. *See also* rift-sawn.

Rift-sawn
A term used to describe a piece of wood with growth rings that meet the faces of the board at angles of more than 30 degrees but at less than 60 degrees.

Rotary-cut
A term used to describe a continuous sheet of veneer peeled from a log by turning it against a stationary knife.

Sapwood
New wood surrounding the denser heartwood.

Seasoning
Reducing the moisture content of timber.

Short grain
A term used to describe where the general direction of wood fibres lies across a narrow section of timber.

Slash-sawn
Another term for plain-sawn.

Softwood
Wood cut from coniferous trees which belong to the botanical group Gymnospermae.

Springwood
Another term for earlywood.

Straight grain
Grain that aligns with the main axis of a workpiece or tree.

Stringing
Fine strips of wood used to divide areas of veneer.

Summerwood
Another term for latewood.

Tangentially cut
Another term for plain-sawn.

Veneer
A thin slice of wood used as a surface covering on a less expensive material such as a man-made board.

Vertical grain
Another term for quarter-sawn.

Wavy grain
A term used to describe the even wave-like grain pattern on wood cut from a tree with an undulating cell structure.

Wild grain
Irregular grain that changes direction, making it difficult to work.

Winding
A warped or twisted board is said to be winding or in wind.